THE ART EXPERIENCE

BY WILLET RYDER, Ed.D.

GoodYearBooks

An Imprint of ScottForesman
A Division of HarperCollins*Publishers*

Dedication

*To Elé and Tama Ryder for their
encouragement and Louise Smith
Ryder for her inspiration*

Good Year Books
are available for preschool through grade 6 for
every basic curriculum subject plus many enrichment
areas. For more Good Year Books, contact your local
bookseller or educational dealer. For a complete catalog
with information about other Good Year Books, please write:

Good Year Books
Scott, Foresman and Company
1900 East Lake Avenue
Glenview, IL 60025

Introduction

The Art Experience is primarily intended for teachers and prospective teachers of the upper elementary grades. It contains a collection of art activities that I have tried and tested in the classroom and have used successfully during the past twenty years. One of the most important aspects of the book is that every idea presented is an open-ended idea; by this, I mean that there is no one "right" way to achieve success. Instead, each activity in this collection encourages the individual to think of his/her own way to reach a solution.

This book is divided into three distinct parts: "Exploring the Self—Learning Who You Are," "The World Around Us," and "Adventures in Design." Each part focuses on a different aspect of the visual arts and contains a particular emphasis.

Part I advances the idea of discovering more about one's own identity through the art process. One of the most vital missions of education is to build a strong sense of self in each person who enters the classroom. Art education, with its stress on uniqueness and respect for individuality, holds a key position in bolstering self-esteem. In our present age, which is fraught with the complications and pressures of the technological world, the solace provided by the visual arts is of exceptional importance.

Part II is filled with a variety of ideas concerning different aspects of our physical world. There is a strong emphasis on art history and visual works representing many cultures of the earth. Learning about one's ties to people from other times and other places is a foundation stone of this section. Participants will become acquainted with a wide range of concepts, such as the "talisman" in Ojo de Dios, the Zen philosophy behind Sumi-E painting, and the tribal ideas connected to ceremonial masks. They will be encouraged to become more careful observers and learn to notice some of the wonderful details that fill our world.

The third and final part concentrates on individual imagination. It challenges each person to delve into his/her own storehouse of fun and fantasy and come up with unique and creative solutions. In this part, the participant will be called upon to think up new ways of doing things. He or she will be invited to explore new paths and trails, which are found only on one's creative road map.

The activities included represent both old ideas and new ideas. Some have been used by art educators for decades, while others are just being tried. The prime consideration is that art can help each individual find success and fulfillment, and that the joy of creativity can truly enhance human life.

Contents

Part Three
Adventures in Design **95**

Part One

Exploring the Self—

Learning Who You Are

The quest to gain a more thorough knowledge of who we are and what we're about is the primary goal of the education process. It is, in fact, the basic place to begin our explorations in art, for by looking more closely into ourselves, we can gain valuable insights into what makes us the unique beings that we are. At the same time, by pursuing such self-investigation, we can also become more sensitized to some of the vital issues and concerns of others.

In this group of art activities, we will be recording visual information about ourselves. We will be describing our feelings to one another and showing who we are through visual means. We will be telling about those people who influence our lives and about the dreams and goals that we experience and to which we aspire. We will be looking at the ethnic groups to which we belong and learning to develop pride in our heritage.

As we consider these ideas and create our own art, we will be on our way to discovering some wonderful individual treasures. So bring out the art materials and get ready to begin the trip. The map you'll be following on this special journey is written in you!

Communicating Feelings

Developing Emotional Insights

Purpose: *To convey a personal feeling in visual form*

Materials:

An assortment of wood and fabric scraps, drawing and construction paper (12" x 18"), cardboard, plasticine, white glue, scissors, tempera paints, brushes, pencils, crayons, markers, newspaper.

Description: *Each of us experiences a wide variety of feelings on a daily basis. One of the greatest qualities of human life is that we all have feelings and that we can share these feelings with others. By attempting to depict an important personal feeling in visual form, one is asked to reflect on that feeling and ponder how to show it to others. This activity invites the students to do just that.*

1 Begin this activity by holding a short discussion on feelings and why they are important. Make a list of feelings that the students have suggested.

2 Ask each student to recall one of his/her personal feelings and make a drawing, painting, collage, or sculpture about it.

3 Be certain to stress that the visual expression of a feeling can be done in whatever style the individual wishes. It can be abstract, realistic, expressionistic, symbolic, simple, or complicated. It is up to each student to decide how to depict this feeling to others.

4 At this point, make a variety of art materials available to the students. Place boxes or bins of different art materials on a table at the front of the room, and let the students make individual selections.

5 Allow the students to work for as long as possible without interruption.

6 After cleaning up, hold a "sharing session." Such a session is of great importance, since it affords each student the opportunity to show and explain his/her art. It is also acceptable if a student does not wish to show or discuss his/her work.

Notes: *Creating an artwork about a personal feeling is a thoughtful and fascinating activity that can aid each student in gaining greater self-knowledge. I have found that initially many students will sit and think for quite some time before starting to work. Perhaps this is a natural reaction to being asked to do such an artwork!*

Once the students have started to work, please try not to interfere. I have found that if students need help, they will ask for it. Since this is a very personal activity, the less interference the better. I am constantly amazed at the wide variety of art that is stimulated by such an activity. In addition to the exciting visual work, the teacher can learn a great deal by hearing the explanations given by the students.

Creative Autobiographies

Celebrating Who You Are

Purpose: *To create a unique work of art that relates important information about your life*

4

Materials:
Manila, white drawing, and colored construction paper (12" x 18"), cardboard, plasticine, wood and fabric scraps, hangers and yarn, pencils, crayons, markers, tempera paints, brushes, scissors, newspaper.

Description: *Who are you? What are you about? What kinds of things do you like? These are some of the questions on which this activity focuses. The main idea is for each student to present important aspects or characteristics of him/herself in a visual work. The work can be in the form of a collage, montage, drawing, painting, sculpture, construction, or mobile. It can be very tiny or very large. The crucial thing is that it must be thoughtful, and it must attempt to describe the individual in some way.*

1 Launch this activity with your class by discussing the meaning of "autobiographies" and the important questions listed above. Explain that in this activity, each child will be asked to make a unique piece of art that tells about her/himself. These works can be done in any style or materials that the students wish to use.

2 Next, invite the students to reflect on themselves and to begin formulating how they plan to explain themselves visually to the class.

3 When each student is ready, ask him/her to select the materials that he/she wishes to use. Have all the materials available on a table in one section of the room, and be sure you have an ample supply. Since many kinds of materials may be needed by the students, it is a good idea to have a number of cardboard storage boxes filled with a variety of items.

4 Be available to encourage the students, answer questions, and give advice about individual problems as they arise.

5 When all the works are complete, hold a sharing session and exhibition. I am confident that you will find this activity to be enlightening for both the students and the teacher.

Notes: *I was first introduced to this activity in one of Victor D'Amico's art education classes about twenty years ago. Over the years, I have used it to start my art classes—whether they be composed of children or adults—for the activity provides an excellent method for students to get better acquainted with themselves and others.*

Looking back over many autobiographical sessions, I find that two creations stick out in my mind. The first of these was a sweater-like garment of yarn, which the student created and wore to class. Pinned to this garment, at various intervals, were about thirty 3" x 5" cards with descriptive words, such as "cheerful," lettered on them. These words expressed the many personality attributes of the student.

The second example was very small and very clever. It consisted of an egg shell that had been cleaned out and carefully cut in half. Stuffed inside the shell was a bunch of colored confetti-like paper with typed messages describing the person. The student explained her project to the class by stating that she was like an egg. Although she was quiet, reserved, and mysterious on the outside, she was filled with all kinds of colorful qualities on the inside!

Depicting Others

Creating Art About Other People

Purpose: *To draw, paint, or sculpt an important person one knows*

6

Materials:
Various sizes of white and manila drawing paper, plasticine, Styrofoam and fabric scraps, pipe cleaners, white glue, scissors, watercolors, tempera paints, brushes, pencils, markers, crayons, plastic cups, water, newspaper.

Description: *People are social beings, and most of us come into contact with a variety of other folks on a daily basis. Family members and close friends are probably the most popular subjects for this activity. However, clergy, teachers, and doctors may also pop up.*

1 This activity should begin with a discussion about the important people we know. Students can make their own lists, or you can write a large list on the chalkboard as the students make their suggestions.

2 Explain to the class that throughout the ages artists have often used other people as the basis for their artwork. You might obtain a general survey book on art history and select some examples that illustrate this fact. Large art prints or slides would be ideal. It is very important to let the students know that there is no "right" way to draw, paint, or sculpt someone. (Several examples from art history should illustrate this point!)

3 Next, ask each student to select one very special person in his/her life and begin to make an artwork about this person. Make available a wide range of art materials for this purpose.

4 Allow the students as much time as possible so they can think and work carefully.

5 After students complete their art, hold a "sharing session." This will provide them with an opportunity to talk about and share their artwork.

Notes: *Although the artwork is important and interesting to see, I believe that the "thinking" is the most significant part of this activity. By focusing on an important person in his/her life, each student will begin to realize why that other person is so special. Such an activity can increase one's understanding of the vital role that others play in our lives.*

Dreams

Purpose: *To explore a dream and show it in an artwork*

Materials:
Crayons,
watercolors,
tempera paints,
brushes,
white drawing paper
(12" x 18" and
larger),
newsprint,
wood and fabric
scraps,
scissors,
white glue,
plasticine,
plastic cups,
water,
newspaper.

Description: *The world of dreams is an exciting place! It is a world filled with many emotions and colors. A wide variety of feelings, such as joy, fear, delight, and suspense, abound. In addition, dreams can also consist of goals or objectives that people are trying to reach. The dreams of John F. Kennedy, Martin Luther King, Jr., or Eleanor Roosevelt are fine examples.*

1 Begin this activity by holding a discussion on dreams. Ask each student to recall an important dream that he/she has experienced. It can be either a dream from one's subconscious world (sleep) or one's conscious world (goals). If you have books or prints about the Surrealists, such as Dali, Magritte, or Miro, this would be an ideal time to show and discuss them.

2 After students have selected a specific dream, have them make some sketches, in any style they wish, and choose their favorites.

3 Each student will then use his/her sketch as the basis for creating the final artwork out of the various materials you make available.

4 After the students complete their work, hold a sharing session.

Notes: *Although it is important to give the students time to consider their dreams, too much time can be detrimental. I have found that spontaneity is a prime ingredient in this activity. It is also a good idea to offer a choice of both two- and three-dimensional materials. This is especially valuable, since not everyone thinks or works well in the same art materials.*

I have had students depict a startling event or a lonely feeling, while others have painted or sculpted a goal for which they are striving or their view for a better world. Whatever the outcome, this activity provides a chance for each student to examine another facet of him/herself more closely. Through a "sharing session," the entire group can get a clearer picture of what each class member is about.

9 ♥

Ethnic Investigations

An Art Accent on Heritage

Purpose: *To clarify an aspect of one's ethnic background through art*

Materials:

White drawing paper (12" x 18" or larger), newsprint, assorted construction paper, cardboard, fabric scraps, yarn, wood scraps, plasticine, scissors, white glue, pencils, crayons, markers, tempera paints, watercolors, brushes, plastic cups, water, newspaper.

Description: *America is like a vast and intricate mosaic composed of many types of pieces. Each type, in turn, possesses a distinct ethnic heritage that connects it to a particular country or group. In this activity, the students will be asked to consider carefully their distinct ethnicity and to create works of art that reflect some aspect of that ethnicity.*

1 You might start the activity by discussing the idea of America. Who were the original Americans? Why does our country motivate immigrants from around the world? What places do Americans come from? Who can name some countries? Where did your parents, grandparents, and great-grandparents come from?

2 Next, point out that people from different parts of the world have different cultures. Different languages, art, music, stories, dances, customs, clothing, and religions are but some of the many things that make each of us a unique person. Ask each student in your class to jot down something about his/her own ethnic heritage on a piece of notebook paper.

Since we are dealing with the visual arts, you may wish to show a selection of art books, slides, or real cultural art from various parts of the world. You may, in fact, have your own collection. Of course, using your own ethnicity will be both valuable and intriguing to your students.

3 Once the children have decided on a subject, encourage them to create their own artwork based on their choice. Make available a wide variety of art materials for this activity. In addition, try to provide everyone with ample working time. You should be available during this time for individual guidance.

4 After the students have completed their artwork, hold a heritage session. Each class member should be given time to explain his/her artwork and answer any questions that may arise. To further enhance the activity, hold a "Heritage Day." Such a day can include visits and stories by parents and grandparents, music, dancing, and various ethnic foods.

Notes: *This activity provides an excellent method for promoting multicultural and multiethnic education. It enables each student to share a portion of his/her own ethnic background and to develop an understanding of the backgrounds of others. In an age of pluralistic education, such an activity clearly illustrates the fact that people are a fascinating curriculum source. As our world becomes smaller and smaller, this activity enables us to appreciate diversity, while, at the same time, learning to cherish all we share as inhabitants of the earth.*

Heraldry

Your Family Crest

Purpose: *To design and create your individual family crest*

Materials:
Manila and white drawing paper (9" x 12"), pencils, markers, crayons, watercolors, brushes, rulers, compasses, plastic cups, water, newspaper.

Description: *During the Middle Ages in Europe, the use of armor encouraged a new area of artistic decoration known as "heraldry." Heraldry refers to the use of visual symbols as identification markers for knights, who were clad from head to toe in metal suits. Without such markings, it would have been extremely difficult to determine who anyone was on a field of battle.*

As time passed and the Middle Ages became history, people began using heraldric crests as family trademarks. These crests usually included shields and armored helmets, along with fanciful floral and animal motifs.

1 Before introducing this activity to your class, check the library and locate several books on heraldry and the Middle Ages. It is also a good idea to get a few books on naming children, since they often have interesting material. If you know your family crest, you should use it in connection with this activity.

2 Bring these materials to class to show to the children, and start a discussion on heraldry. Why do you think this art form developed? What does it have to do with armor? Discuss the fact that if armor and shields did not have special visual symbols, people would have difficulty recognizing one another.

12

3 Explain that in this activity, each of the students will be designing his/her own family crest. Crests may depict either the first or last names. Students can consult the books that you have collected. Although some children may have family crests of their own, new designs can be based on personal interests and pursuits.

4 Pass out the manila paper and pencils, and have each student make some initial sketches of his/her idea.

5 Next, ask each child to choose his/her favorite design and transfer it to white drawing paper. This design can then be completed using colored markers and watercolors. The students may also wish to letter their names beneath their crests, using guidelines.

6 Hold a final sharing session and show at the conclusion of the activity.

Notes: *I have found that this activity always intrigues students. Over the years, children have created some marvelous designs based on both names and interests. I have seen leaping swordfish, wonderful flowers and plants, cars, mountains, banners, and crowns. Children seem to take off with the idea that their names are important. Indeed, many students have framed their crests to better display them at home. This activity provides a fine opportunity for each individual to not only create an exciting personal symbol, but also to bolster her/his self-esteem.*

Name Designs

Your Personal Label

Purpose: *To create a unique visual design based on your name*

14
♥

Materials:
Newsprint and white drawing paper (9" x 12"), pencils, markers, crayons, watercolors, brushes, rulers, compasses, plastic cups, water, newspaper.

Description: *Your name, whether it is your first or last name, is one of the most significant visual symbols used to identify you. In this activity, we will be focusing on our names and creating special designs about them.*

1 Begin this activity by explaining to the students that they will be creating name designs. Discuss the fact that such designs can be connected to an individual's personal interests and concerns. For example, if one of the children loves football, he/she may wish to create letters using tiny footballs.

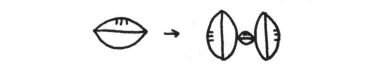

Be sure to mention to the students that each letter, regardless of its style, should be drawn with dimension, rather than in a single line, as shown below. This will enable each child to add additional decoration and interest to their design.

Pass out the newsprint and pencils, and ask the students to make a number of sketches using their names.

 Next, ask each child to select his/her favorite sketch and transfer it to the white drawing paper using pencil. Students should be allowed to use rulers and compasses if they so desire.

4 After they have transferred the designs, they can decorate them using crayons, markers, and watercolors.

5 When the final designs are complete, hold a sharing session and exhibit.

Notes: *"Name Designs" are an excellent method for getting to know your students better. Since the focus is specifically directed to the individual's name, each child can very easily become personally involved. In this sense, the activity is both thought-provoking and fun.*

My favorite aspect of "Name Designs" is that they make each person feel important. By giving our attention to our own personal label, each of us is affirming, in a visual manner, our own identity. This is a fine activity to introduce to your class at the beginning of the school year.

Self-Portraits

Here's Looking at You!

Purpose: *Learning to look at oneself more closely*

16

♥

Materials:
Pencils, charcoal, newsprint, manila or white drawing paper (12" x 18"), small mirrors.

Description: *Self-portraits have appeared in art throughout the ages. Many artists have not only used themselves as subjects, but have, like Rembrandt, worn special costumes for the occasion. In this activity, the students will be asked to study themselves and make drawings based on these studies.*

1 To start the activity, hold a discussion about self-portraits. To enhance your talk, show some examples from art history. Be sure, however, that the examples you choose represent a variety of styles.

2 Next, distribute paper, pencils, charcoal, and mirrors to your students. Each individual should have his/her own small mirror. Ask the children to spend a few moments looking carefully at their faces in the mirrors. Encourage them to pay particular attention to the distinctive features of their faces.

3 After this is done, they should begin drawing. Have the students do the first drawing without looking at their papers. Then have them do a second drawing, consulting both the mirror and the paper. It is important for them to take their time and really look! Explain to the students that self-portraits do not have to be realistic. They can be done in any artistic style, but they should reflect some quality that the student noticed in his/her face. For example, if a student has very large eyes, they should be emphasized in the self-portrait.

4 To make this activity more dramatic, pull down the shades or blinds in your classroom and turn on a very limited amount of overhead lighting. The shadows that are created will emphasize each face in a different way. Ask the children to use charcoal and try to shade their drawings as shown in the mirrors.

5 After the students complete the drawings, discuss the self-portraits. You might see who can guess the person from the portrait.

Notes: *Self-portraits can be challenging for the children and can provide them with a great method for increasing personal observation. Often we look only superficially at our faces, without really seeing what's there. By asking your students to study what they look like and to depict something of this look, you can help them to "see" more clearly.*

Zodiac Designs

Everyone Can Be a Star!

Purpose: *To create a visual design based on one's astrological sign*

Materials:
Large sheets of
white drawing paper
or watercolor
paper,
newsprint
(12" x 18" or larger),
pencils,
markers,
watercolors,
tempera paints,
brushes,
plastic cups,
water,
newspaper.

Description: *Human beings have always been curious about the stars! It was the ancient Greeks, however, who devised twelve visual symbols to identify the various constellations that represent the zodiac signs. Each zodiac sign not only has its own unique symbol, but it also corresponds to a particular time on the calendar when this special constellation appears in the night sky. These signs relate both to astronomy (the scientific study of the stars and other heavenly bodies) and astrology (the idea of foretelling future events by studying the influence of star, moon, and sun positions on human affairs).*

1 Discuss the zodiac, astronomy, and astrology with your students. You might bring in a newspaper and posters to enhance your discussion. Then have each student determine his/her own zodiac sign according to date of birth.

2 Next, using the newsprint as sketch paper, encourage each student to develop a group of sketches depicting his/her own sign. It is important to tell the students to use whatever style they wish in creating their art.

3 After each student has selected his/her favorite sketch, he/she will then use pencil to transfer it to a large sheet of white drawing paper or watercolor paper.

4 Students then color the completed pencil drawing using markers, watercolors, or tempera paints. A combination of these materials is also very effective.

5 Hold a presentation session at the conclusion of the activity, when the completed artwork can be shown and discussed. Several sessions may be needed to enable the students to complete their designs.

Notes: *"Zodiac Designs" are a great springboard into many subject areas. Through individual investigation of the various constellations, students can gain some fine insights into astronomy. They might also enjoy reading the astrology pages in the local newspaper—just for fun! Perhaps, most significantly, each student will have another creative experience and visual record celebrating his/her own unique identity.*

Over the years, I have found that this activity is a wonderful way for kids to get involved in something about themselves. I also feel that working on large paper is a real asset for this activity. Perhaps because stars and constellations are so vast in size, the large designs are especially exciting for students.

Part Two

The World Around Us

Our world is a marvelous storehouse of objects and ideas—a place of amazement and delight. Since there is such great diversity within it, we will only sample some of the many wonders that are waiting for us outside our windows and doors. We will wander along beaches and down the roads of our neighborhoods. We will travel, through art experience, to different points around our planet. We will draw landscapes and sculpt objects from wood and sand. We will interpret past events and focus on diverse cultural offerings. We will develop puppet characters and learn simple weaving. In short, we will try to experience a small selection of our world's abundance.

The paths that we follow on this adventure will hopefully stimulate us to become more curious about things in our environment. In this respect, although the art activities are visually and creatively oriented, they are designed to tempt us to investigate further in other realms. Social studies, language arts, and science are also very much connected to this investigation. As we take part in each activity, we will all gain greater wisdom about the wonders of the world around us.

Crayon Etching

Just a Scratch of Color

Purpose: *To develop an appreciation for the technique of etching*

22

Materials:

Crayon and crayon scraps,
White drawing paper (9" x 12"),
dried-out ballpoint pens,
nails,
newspapers,
newsprint or manila sketch paper.

Description: *Colored lines and designs springing magically from a waxy black background—this is the initial impression of a crayon etching.*

1 Begin this activity by holding a brief discussion about etchings. What is an etching? Explain that although etchings are usually done on metal and glass, which have been coated with wax, they can also be done on paper. In both situations, a sharp object is used to do the drawing. You may also wish to show and discuss examples of actual etchings.

2 Next, explain that we will be creating "crayon etchings," and have your students gather around for a demonstration. Start by covering your paper with different areas of well-crayoned strips, bands, or squares. The number of colors chosen is up to the individual creator. If you leave a white border of about 1" around the edge of your paper, it will provide an unwaxed area, enabling you to hold the paper more securely. Since the next step is quite messy, it is wise to cover your desk or table top with newspaper, which will enable easy clean-up.

3 After the paper has been richly colored (eliminate all empty spots), it is time to cover the colored areas with black crayon. During this process, many tiny flakes of crayon will begin to collect around the paper. To facilitate this covering process, you may wish to use a small amount of talcum powder. Spread the powder over the colored areas, and then apply the black crayon.

4 After the paper is completely covered with black, you are ready to begin the actual etching. However, before starting to do this, create a sketch on manila paper or newsprint to use as a guide. Then, using the nails and dry pens, scratch through the black crayon to reveal the rich colors underneath. Through experimentation, you can create many marvelous kinds of lines.

5 After the demonstration, let the children get to work. Once they have completed their etchings, have them share their work with the class and set up a display.

23

Notes: *When I was a small child I sat spellbound as my sister and her friend created a mysterious art form using crayons and nails. I was amazed and excited when they let me try it! I just couldn't believe that you could do such things with crayon. This feeling of amazement is characteristic of crayon etchings.*

It is important to stress that doing crayon etching effectively requires hard work and elbow grease. If the students prepare a nice colored undercoating for their etching, they will be rewarded with a strong and rich-looking work. Therefore, encourage the children to color heavily and take their time. The final results will be well worth the extra effort.

Crayon Resist

Wax and Water Wonders

Purpose: *To develop an appreciation for how varied art materials can interact with one another*

24

Materials:
White drawing paper (12" x 18"),
crayons,
watercolors,
brushes,
water,
plastic cups,
newspaper,
paper towels.

Description: *The world of crayon resist is filled with watery adventure, enhanced by bold lines and subtle washes. It is an exciting place where two media work hand in hand to complement and support one another.*

1 Start this activity by having your students make a crayon drawing on any subject of their choosing. The drawings can be done in any style. The significant thing to remember is that they should leave some white space, and they should not overdo areas of a single crayon color. A mottled semi-crayoned area is actually preferable to an over-crayoned area.

2 After everybody has completed their crayon work, it is time to get out the watercolors. However, before distributing them to the students, it is a good idea to review some basic information about watercolor. You might, in fact, hold a brief watercolor demonstration. In conducting such a session, explain that watercolors should always be moistened before using. A few drops of water, flicked from a wet brush onto each pat of color, is an excellent way to begin. If you want to paint a large area of your paper with a color, it is wise to first paint the area with water and then brush in the color you desire. This technique is called a "wash." If you wish to create a rough, scratchy-looking texture, dry your brush with a paper towel and apply very little paint to the surface of your paper. This technique is known as "dry-brush." After explaining or showing these things to the students, distribute the watercolors.

3 Encourage the students to paint over their crayon drawing using whatever colors and techniques they wish. As they do so, you might question the students about what happens. Since the crayoned areas repel the watercolor, the various areas of uncrayoned paper will pick up the paint, creating amazing results.

4 After the works have been completed, hold a sharing and discussion session, followed by an art exhibit.

Notes: *Once you create a crayon resist, the beauty and excitement of combining crayon and watercolor is immediately evident, for the two media interact very well together. When doing this activity, encourage your students to experiment with different colors and textures. Intricate linear patterns and bold areas of color work are equally effective. Remember, however, that unlike crayon etching, crayon resist needs empty spaces and mottled colored areas in order to be successful. Therefore, it is important to remind your students not to color their original drawing too completely!*

25

Crayon Rubbings

Everything Makes an Impression

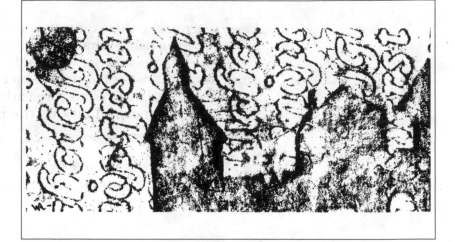

Purpose: *To create designs based on textural impressions*

26

Materials:
*White drawing and
assorted colored
construction paper
(12" x 18"),
crayons,
scissors,
paper scraps,
a wide variety of
textural materials
(cloth scraps, bark,
bits of screening,
sandpaper, etc.).*

Description: *Crayon rubbings are magic! They are an
exciting way to pick up patterns and imprints from our
environment. They are also an excellent way of creating
designs from work that each of us has made. Crayon, a
curious combination of wax and pigment, is perhaps the
most common art material. Although some people scoff at its
simplistic nature, others marvel at the bright colors, slick
texture, and distinctive odor.*

*An activity like "Crayon Rubbings" should be one of
discovery and experimentation. Students should be
encouraged to be explorers, seeking new textures and shapes
to claim for their designs.*

1 A fine way to begin such an activity is to have a
discussion about the many textures in our world.
Encourage your students to look carefully around the
classroom and at their friends. Many objects, including
our clothing, display an exciting range of textures. You
might also show a number of completed crayon
rubbings to stimulate interest.

2 Next, conduct a brief demonstration to illustrate
how easy it is to create a crayon rubbing. Cut out
a shape of any kind from a scrap of paper and place it
under a piece of 12" x 18" paper on your desk, table,
or chalkboard. Then, using the side of your crayon,
rub over the 12" x 18" paper hard enough that the
impression of the shape comes through. It's amazing!

Try the same thing by choosing various objects around the room or from your pocket or purse. The edge of the chalkboard, the light switch, a comb, and a quarter are but a few of the things you might use.

3 Once the students have the idea, have them create their own designs by cutting out their own shapes, choosing objects from the environment, or using a combination of both. Stress the fact that they may also use a variety of colors. Be sure to point out that the side of the crayon works more effectively than the point. Crayons covered with paper should be peeled for better results.

Notes: *It's funny that many students, and teachers too, have only used crayons for coloring-book-type activities. As a result, they are sometimes hesitant to peel off the crayon wrapping and use the side of this exciting art material. In fact, old broken crayons, minus their paper, are excellent for this activity. I always keep a large plastic bin filled with these crayon scraps just for this purpose!*

Try to inspire your students to carefully observe all around them for possible textures and patterns. You might expand the activity into a longer quest by taking a supervised field trip. Old buildings, local cemeteries, manhole covers, and the decorations on automobiles are just some of the possible sources for great crayon rubbings.

Driftwood Sculpture

Letting Your Creativity Branch Out!

Purpose: *To create sculptures suggested by the forms of natural objects*

28

Materials:
*Varied pieces of
driftwood,
new 2' x 4's,
found objects (such
as corks, bottle
caps, or buttons),
nails,
screw eyes,
white glue,
fishline,
coathanger wire,
hammers,
screwdrivers,
coping saws,
files,
tin snips or
wire cutters,
crosscut saw,
sandpaper,
safety goggles,
latex housepaint,
brushes,
plastic cups,
newspapers.*

Description: *Seashores, riverbanks, and lakefronts can provide a wealth of art materials for the classroom. Not only are these materials free, but they are often thought-provoking and challenging to the students. Driftwood is a prime example. Its curious shapes, colors, and textures can provide children with a fascinating art experience. However, the teacher must do some very serious planning for this activity.*

1 Prior to doing the activity, take a scouting expedition to a nearby beach or river bank. It is a handy idea to bring along a few empty cardboard boxes or large reinforced trash bags in which to carry the driftwood. Try to choose pieces of wood that are not too large or bulky, since they may be difficult to transport. A good beach should provide an ample amount of wood very quickly. Generally, I try to gather at least twice the amount of driftwood I need for the class. In this way, every student will have a good choice and can make a second sculpture if they wish.

2 After gathering the driftwood, purchase a few 2' x 4's at a local lumberyard. A single eight-foot length will make many sculpture bases for the finished works. You might also buy a variety of nails and screw eyes.

3 After carting these goodies home, you should make your own sculpture before trying it with your class. Once your driftwood sculpture is completed, you will be better prepared to work with your students.

4 To conduct this activity with your students, place the driftwood pieces in various places around your classroom. Position the pieces under desks, on tabletops, and along window ledges prior to the students' arrival. When they reach the room, explain that you want each child to select a piece of wood that appeals to them.

5 Once each individual has selected his/her piece of wood, encourage him/her to study it carefully. What does it look like? What does it remind them of? What does it suggest? These are some of the crucial questions that should aid the students to focus on their wood pieces more closely.

6 After everyone has decided what they wish to create, it is time to discuss tools and tool safety. You must supervise all tool use carefully. This includes hammering, sawing, and filing. Everyone must always wear safety goggles while using tools.

If the children wish to alter their wood shapes, have them mark the changes they wish to make directly on the driftwood in pencil. They can add other items of interest, such as bottle caps or corks, at this stage using either nails or glue.

7 After all necessary sawing, hammering, and sanding has been completed, the students are ready to mount their sculptures on the 2' x 4' bases. You can cut each base from the 2' x 4' length. The students can file and sand each base to the desired smoothness. They can attach the finished sculptures to the bases with glue, nails, or coathanger wire. You should cut all coathanger wire in straight pieces, using either tin snips or wire cutters.

8 To attach a sculpture to its base by wire, first drive a nail into the base and then remove it. This will create a hole for the wire. The same method should be used on the actual sculpture. Once you have made these holes, drive the wire into them and mount the sculpture onto the base. If the student wishes to suspend his/her sculpture, add a screw eye, attach fishline, and hang the sculpture from the ceiling.

9 Students who wish to paint their sculpture or base should use latex paint, since it is more permanent than tempera.

10 After all the sculptures are completed, hold a sharing session and discussion. Needless to say, this is a longer term activity, which will involve many sessions. However, the students will not only end up with some fantastic results, but they will also develop a better understanding of the many phases that an artwork of this type must go through.

Notes: *The excitement of driftwood sculptures is well worth the extra effort. I must stress that safety procedures must be carefully explained and followed at all times. The use of safety goggles while working with tools is imperative!*

Once the students have begun this activity, you will find that they won't want to stop. A wide variety of plant, animal, bird, and free forms should result. I have found that the students especially enjoy sanding and refining their shapes. In addition, most children seem to develop a sharper eye for some of the many beautiful things that our natural environment offers us. Such sculptures provide a real connection to environmental studies and ecology.

Figure Drawing

The Power of People

Purpose: *To increase the power of observation by teaching one to look more carefully*

Materials:
*Pencils,
ballpoint pens,
markers,
crayons,
newsprint or manila
paper (12" x 18" or
larger).*

Description: *The human figure has always intrigued and mystified us, whether we view the early stick figures of young children or the sophisticated renderings of adult artists. Throughout history, it has been incised into walls, etched in metal and glass, painted on canvas, drawn on paper, and woven into tapestries. It is a universal symbol of the human condition, understood despite time and cultural differences.*

Everyone likes to draw people, but most of us are timid about it. Children, however, especially in the mid-elementary grades, can be easily convinced to try some drawing exercises

1 In beginning this activity, remember to point out to the students that any style of drawing is acceptable. The activity should, in fact, stress experimentation and freedom. Since we are trying to increase the ability to observe, it is important to have an actual model. Thus, the next order of business is to select a model from the class. There are usually plenty of volunteers! Keep in mind that the models should change often, so that a number of students have a chance and everyone has the opportunity to draw.

2 If your classroom has tables, move a table into the middle of the room and place the other desks or tables around it. If you only have desks, place a few together to form a table-like stand. Ask the model to stand or sit on this elevated central platform. I would also recommend the use of costumes or props to help make the model more interesting. Old hats, a blanket, a broom, a cane, or an umbrella are but a few of the items you can use. Although the class may get a little silly in the beginning, they will get more serious as the activity progresses.

3 Before distributing any supplies, have the model take a pose. Let the model decide what he or she wants to do. Then advise the students to look carefully at the model. Ask them a few questions about what they see. You might also point out particular qualities about the pose that deserve their attention. Once they have their paper and are ready to begin drawing, explain that you want them to look only at the model and not at their paper. They should also use only a single continuous line, not lifting their drawing instrument off the paper.

4 Pass out the art materials, and have the students draw for five minutes. Walk around the room to make sure they aren't peeking at their papers. After five minutes have passed, have the model change poses. Then ask the students to begin another drawing following the same format.

5 After completing several such drawings, have the students start another work. However, on this drawing, allow them to look at their paper, and let them work for fifteen minutes. They can also use broken lines. Explain that they may wish to use some background details or imaginatively change the setting of the model. (For example, they might place him/her in a park, rather than on a table.)

6 At the conclusion of the drawing session, hold a discussion about the work. Ask the children for their reactions, and invite them to show their drawings. Point out that much of drawing is concerned with observation, and that, like swimming, drawing takes practice.

Notes: *No one becomes an artist overnight. It takes work, experimentation, and drive. This activity is a good illustration of these things. It is vital to remember that the activity is designed to encourage better observation. Therefore, the way the drawings look is not as important as what they are attempting to get at!*

Although figure drawing is a popular activity at the high school or college level, it is usually not done in the mid-elementary grades. I feel that this is unfortunate. Children at this level are very interested in trying to draw people, and generally they have a positive attitude about it. This activity is a fine way to get kids involved in the observation business, a crucial ingredient in art.

Found Object Prints

General Impressions

Purpose: *To create printed designs from an assortment of found objects*

34

Materials:
*A variety of found objects,
white and colored construction paper (12" x 18"),
tempera paints (assorted colors),
brushes,
aluminum trays or pie tins,
newspapers,
sponges.*

Description: *Just as people leave footprints when they walk through a puddle, all objects make their own distinct marks after being treated with paint and stamped or rolled onto a surface. One of the challenges of this activity is, in fact, to see how many found objects you can locate as a source of interesting impressions. Long Island sculptor and friend Richard Fleig often supplies me with some wonderful scrap objects from his studio, which are great for this activity.*

1 Search your home and surrounding environment for small objects that appear to have potential as print sources. Clothespins, combs, nails, bottle caps, plastic ware, corks, stones, shells, leaves, sticks, and wood scraps are all wonderful possibilities. Place these objects in a bag for easy access.

2 Next, try a few experimental prints of your own before doing this activity with your class. The procedure is listed below:

a. Choose an interesting object or two from your collection bag.
b. If your work space is not formica or an easy-clean surface, cover it with newspaper.
c. Pour a small amount of tempera paint into an aluminum tray or pie plate, and select the paper on which you wish to do your print.

d. Dip your object(s) or a portion of it into the paint or coat it using a brush, and firmly press it onto your paper. Try experimenting with varying pressure, methods of application, and colors, and be inventive about your design.

e. When the design is dry, you may wish to work over it with impressions from other objects using the same process.

 Bring your object collection and the prints you created to class, and introduce the printing process. Explain that curious prints can be made by using a wide variety of found objects.

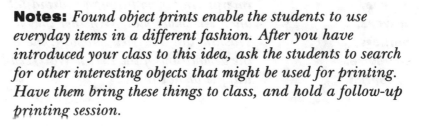 Be sure your students are ready to work with the paint, and ask them to choose a few objects as print sources.

Distribute the paint, trays, brushes, and paper and let them get to work. Be available to answer any questions as they arise.

When all the prints are complete and dry, hold a sharing session and exhibition.

35

Notes: *Found object prints enable the students to use everyday items in a different fashion. After you have introduced your class to this idea, ask the students to search for other interesting objects that might be used for printing. Have them bring these things to class, and hold a follow-up printing session.*

The unusual and intriguing print shapes that result from this activity are always a novelty. Indeed, even the simplest things can make wonderful impressions!

Illustrating Historical Stories

Bringing History Alive Through Art

Purpose: *To reinforce one's understanding of important historical figures and events through the creation of artwork*

36

Materials:
Drawing paper (12" x 18"), pencils, crayons, markers, plasticine, newsprint.

Description: *History, either from the distant past or yesterday, can be enhanced by connecting it to art. By reflecting on significant historical figures and events, and interpreting them through individual art projects, students often remember more. Whether they focus on George Washington, Harriet Tubman, the Battle of Gettysburg, or the demolition of the Berlin Wall, students can provide unique visual input.*

1 To begin this activity, it is best to select a historical figure or issue with plenty of interest. Do some preliminary research, and develop a descriptive essay or story based on the person or the specific event.

2 Read or tell the story to your students, and hold a question and discussion period. Try to refrain from showing illustrations of the person or event during your storytelling. It is best to let the students form their own mental pictures while you tell the tale.

3 At the conclusion of your narrative, ask the students to draw or sculpt the person or event you have just described. Provide them with the materials, stand back, and let them get to work. You should be available, however, to answer any questions that may arise.

4 When students have completed their artwork, hold a sharing session and display.

Notes: *The high degree of imagination and whimsy that children bring to such an activity never ceases to amaze me. I have seen serious Martin Luther Kings, happy Sacajeweas, tricky Ferdinands and Isabellas, and a slew of unusual ships, castles, and cities. All of these things are based on real people and occurrences. However, the children's viewpoints are forever new, fresh, and exciting. I would recommend such an activity as a viable way to help revitalize a social studies lesson.*

My wife, Eleanor Ryder, often has her fourth-grade class create large cut-paper people whom they are studying. Since she is very interested in famous women, her classes have created and learned a great deal employing this method. Once the children have created their artwork, it is a good idea to provide relevant books and articles, which they can consult for further study.

37

Kites

Light and Breezy Designs

Purpose: *To design and create a decorative kite, inspired by nature or imagination*

Materials:
*Newsprint,
wallpaper scraps,
colored
construction paper,
yarn,
fishing line,
assorted found
objects (such as
buttons,
plastic eyes, etc.),
markers,
scissors,
hole punch.*

Description: *When the breeze is brisk and the sky is clear, the idea of flying a kite often springs to mind. Kites, however, don't have to be flown to be interesting. The fact is that the exciting designs of some kites (like the wonderful Chinese peacock kite that my daughter received from her uncle) make them fascinating visual objects for decorating houses and schools. In this activity, the focus will be on designing kites for decorative purposes rather than for flight.*

1 A good way to initiate this activity is to bring in some actual kites so that the class can see and discuss them. If your community has a hobby or craft shop, this may be a place to locate examples. Some Oriental gift shops stock a selection of kites also. Of course, if you aren't able to find some sample kites, you can always create your own.

2 After showing the kites, explain that the class will be concerned with making decorative kites rather than kites for flight. Ask your students for their ideas about the forms that decorative kites might take. Could they represent birds, animals, or insects? How about plants or imaginary creatures? Make a list on the chalkboard of the suggestions that the children come up with.

38

3 Once the list is quite long, have each child select a topic (such as a butterfly), and make a sketch on newsprint to help visualize his/her idea. If they need some additional information about what a particular animal or plant looks like, give them an encyclopedia or nature book.

4 When each child has a completed sketch, it is time to begin the actual construction of the kite. A wide range of two-dimensional materials should be on hand for this purpose. Wallpaper samples are excellent materials for the basic kite shapes. Try to encourage the students to make their kites quite large, since they are easier to work on and more exciting to display.

5 If the kite shape is symmetrical, students can more easily make it by folding and cutting. Fish, insects, stars, and leaves are but a few such examples. Extra decorative touches can be added by using colored construction paper, yarn, or buttons. Make sure that the children use glue instead of staples to attach their decorations, since it looks more polished.

6 After the kites are complete, students can discuss and display them. You might exhibit them either as mobiles or on bulletin boards.

39

Notes: *Since wallpaper is a valuable material in this activity, as well as in some others, it's a good idea to acquaint yourself with the local wallpaper store. Explain your mission to the salesperson, and see if he/she is willing to donate some wallpaper sample books to your class. If you are given some free materials, be sure to make a follow-up visit or phone call to express your appreciation. I have become friendly with a local wallpaper salesperson, who now calls me when she wishes to dispose of sample books. Although the creation of the kites is fun, the exhibition of them is equally exciting. Over the years, I have developed an easy approach to a suspended mobile-type exhibit. First, fit each kite with yarn or fishing line by punching a hole with the punch and knotting on the line. At the opposite end of the line, tie a loop and add a paper clip. To hang the kite, open the clip slightly and rest it on the end of a yardstick. Lift the line, with the kite attached, using the yardstick, until*

the open paper clip is just above the light fins of most school lighting. Then carefully bring the yardstick down until the clip and attached kite are supported by the light fin.

By using this method, you can hang any number of kites without the use of a chair, desk, or ladder. To take down the exhibit, merely slide the clips off the light fins using your yardstick. Within a short time, the classroom can be transformed into a kite display shop. (Watch the length of the yarn or line so that it is above head level.) Needless to say, the air motion from general room use will move the kites in mobile fashion!

40

Landscapes

Just Outside the Door

Purpose: *To develop awareness and appreciation of the physical environment in which we live*

Materials:
Newsprint and white drawing paper (12" x 18"), pencils, crayons, corrugated cardboard pieces (14" x 20"), water bucket, paper towels, watercolors, brushes, plastic cups, water, newspaper, picnic blankets, large plastic trash bags, shopping bags.

Description: *When I think of landscapes, I think of tremendous diversity. Whether one focuses on the deserts of Israel, the mountains of New Zealand, the wheat fields of Kansas, or the streets of New York City, the landscapes of the world are characterized by great variety and interest. In this activity, the key factor is to stimulate your students to notice and study what surrounds them.*

1 Start this activity by telling your students that you will be taking a short trip, just outside the school, in order to draw and paint the area. You don't have to travel far to find challenging things to draw. The school playground will probably be adequate. In the event of poor weather, encourage your children to position themselves near a window and draw the landscape outside.

If you go outside, please plan ahead to have blankets or pieces of plastic sheeting for the children to sit on. By asking the students to bring in picnic blankets ahead of time, you will be all set when the actual day arrives.

2 After the students have selected a place to camp or a window to sit by, they are ready to begin looking and recording. Each person should be given art materials at this time. As the students begin to work, keep in mind that the drawing is not as important as the seeing, for the crucial idea is to get the children to really look at the environment. In addition, a wide range of approaches and styles should be evident. For example, while one student may focus on trying to render a row of apartments behind the school, another may be concentrating on showing the bold geometric shapes on one of the buildings.

3 Let the students work for a while in pencil on newsprint. (Rest the newsprint against the larger piece of corrugated cardboard.) Then encourage them to transfer their drawings to white drawing paper and begin to use crayons and watercolors. To transport these art materials more easily, use shopping bags with handles. Don't forget to bring along a bucket of water and a bag of plastic cups to hold the water for each painter. It is also a wise idea to have plenty of paper towels available for wiping brushes and hands.

4 Once students have completed the artworks and cleaned up the materials, it is time to return to the classroom. Hold a sharing session at this time.

Notes: *This activity might be a fine time to introduce the idea of sketchbooks to your students. These handy sketch diaries are an indispensable tool for the artist and avid observer. Suggest that when children go on vacations, they bring along a sketchbook as they would bring along a camera, for such a book, especially if small in size, can be carried easily in a knapsack or small bag.*

This kind of activity will no doubt contain a number of pleasant surprises for students and teachers alike. Indeed, the landscape drawings usually illustrate the diverse viewpoints of children. No matter how many times I introduce this activity, I always learn new ways of seeing from my students!

Cardboard Masks

The Power of the False Face

Purpose: *To design and create a decorative mask*

Materials:

Newsprint or manila paper,

corrugated cardboard,

colored construction paper,

paper scraps,

assorted yarn,

feathers,

buttons,

glue,

scissors,

markers,

crayons,

tempera paints,

brushes,

plastic cups,

water,

newspaper.

Description: *Whenever children hear the word "masks," most automatically think of Halloween. Yet masks can serve purposes other than covering the faces of trick or treaters. In this activity, we will focus on the design and construction of decorative masks.*

1 Begin this activity by obtaining books from the library on any of the following: African art, Native American art, Eskimo art, art of Southeast Asia and Japan, art of the South Pacific, or Mexican art. These are but a few of the topics that spring to mind in connection with decorative ceremonial masks. Of course, if you are lucky enough to own some of these masks, it would be fine to show them to your students later.

It is also wise to gather the corrugated cardboard at this time. Supermarkets are an excellent source for obtaining cardboard boxes. Take the boxes apart and cut them into flat pieces using a mat or art knife.

2 Next, present your examples to the students, and hold a discussion on some of the purposes for masks. Through talking with the children, establish the idea that masks can be tied to religious events, magical rites, and natural forces. In some cultures, they can also symbolize links to ancestors and to birds and animals. Some masks are quite realistic, while others are very abstract. In addition, masks can reflect any number of emotions from humor to surprise.

3 After the children have had an opportunity to see and discuss masks, explain that they will be creating their own decorative, ceremonial mask. Point out that since the mask is decorative, it will not be designed for wear, but rather for display. Ask each student to develop some ideas through drawing on newsprint or manila paper. You might also have some of the library books available for the children to consult.

4 Once the children have decided upon the design they wish to use, they are ready to begin working with the cardboard. Explain that they can peel the cardboard to reveal the corrugations, and they can build it up, like building blocks, into a number of layers. Distribute the cardboard and have them draw their designs and begin cutting.

Although cardboard is not easy to cut, the children can plow their way through it by using ordinary school scissors. *Do not* allow them to use art knives, mat cutters, or razor blades! By taking their time, and carefully cutting, peeling, building up, and gluing the cardboard, they can achieve some very fascinating results.

5 After they have cut and glued the basic cardboard shapes, the children are ready to decorate and embellish their masks with a wide range of scrap paper, buttons, yarn, feathers, and found objects. They can also use crayons, markers, and tempera paints. After they have finished decorating the masks, dry the artwork thoroughly.

6 Hold a final sharing session, where the children can show and tell about their masks. A follow-up exhibit in the hallways or school library is a fine conclusion for such an activity.

44

Notes: *Elementary students seem to be natural mask makers. Their strong sense of uninhibited design and emotion is always shown effectively in their works. I have found ordinary corrugated cardboard to be excellent for such an activity, since it appears to be very wood-like. By peeling off the top layer to expose the corrugations, and by building it to various heights, you can create some wonderful effects.*

Although many materials are great for decoration, colored feathers are especially appealing to the children. Thus, in recent years, I have made a special effort to purchase a variety of feathers for this activity. I have found that feathers can often be purchased through large floral supply houses, which sell to local florists. Check the yellow pages in your area for such suppliers. These suppliers often stock a multitude of beads, artificial fur, and other materials. If your school has a tax-free number, you will not pay sales tax, and you may also get an additional discount.

45

Paper Masks

Facing New Possibilities

Purpose: *To design and create simple construction paper masks*

46

Materials:
*Colored construction paper (12" x 18"),
paper scraps,
glue,
markers,
crayons,
scissors,
hole punch,
assorted found objects,
string or elastic.*

Description: *A simple sheet of paper can be turned into some exciting things! This statement characterizes the creation of paper masks. Such masks can be worn and/or used for decoration. They are easy to make, and they provide the students ample opportunity to demonstrate a wide range of creative ideas.*

1 A discussion of masks and mask-making is always a nice way to begin such a lesson. You might also wish to elicit possible mask themes from the students. List them on the board. Various animals, birds, insects, and monsters are a few examples. Show some masks at this time, and explain that masks need not be worn, but they can be used for decoration.

2 Next, demonstrate two approaches for constructing a simple paper mask. The two approaches are:

The Rectangular Mask: After selecting a theme, take a 12″ x 18″ sheet of construction paper and fold it down the center (the long way), creating two 6″ x 18″ segments. Cut a nose and mouth by holding the fold and cutting half of each shape.

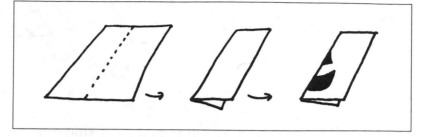

Now fold the paper into quarter segments (the long way), creating four 3″ x 18″ segments. Cut out the eyes by using the same method as for the nose and mouth.

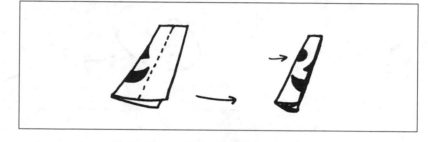

Once these cuts are completed, unfold and flatten out the paper. Then make four diagonal cuts, about 3″ in length, in the corners of the paper.

 Slide each of the cut corner tabs past one another until the mask begins to stand up. Then glue or staple each corner until all four corners have been completed. The mask, which will now appear more three-dimensional, is ready to receive extra decoration and enrichment.

The Circular Mask: Once the theme has been selected, fold and cut the rectangular piece of paper into a circular shape.

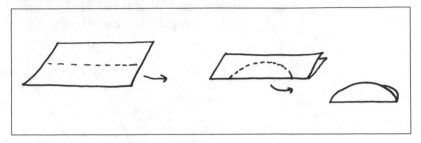

Next, cut the circular shape halfway up the fold, and slide and overlap the two cut segments until the shape appears cone-like. Glue or staple the edges to hold this shape.

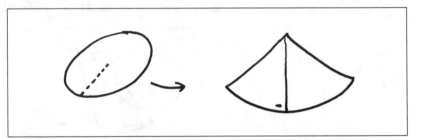

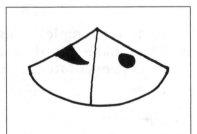

Cut out eyes and mouths after making the cone shape. Gently punch into the cone, and cut out the desired shapes. Attach additional decorations.

3 After completing your demonstration, distribute materials to the students so that they can begin to work. Once they complete the masks, punch two holes at the sides and attach a thin piece of elastic or string. The masks can then be worn, displayed, and discussed.

Notes: *Perhaps the high point of excitement in this activity is the realization by the children that a flat sheet of paper can be changed into a three-dimensional shape. Once they understand this information, the children will begin to think of all sorts of relief-like additions to their masks. Keep in mind that a simple tab folded at the base of a paper decoration will make gluing easier. By adding paper noses, eyelashes, hair, and teeth, the children will learn new ways to work, and, no doubt, demonstrate plenty of original ideas.*

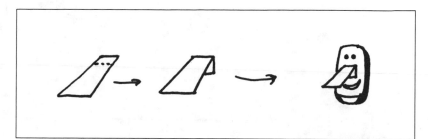

Mobiles

Miraculous Moving Machines

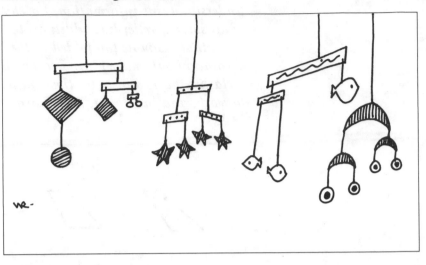

Purpose: *To learn about and construct a movable suspended sculpture*

50

Materials:
*Newsprint,
cardboard,
fishing line,
heavy-duty thread,
colored
construction paper,
found objects,
pencils,
markers,
glue,
scissors,
hole punch,
tempera paints,
brushes,
plastic cups,
water,
newspaper.*

Description: *Leaves move, branches shake, clouds sail, water rushes, and people and animals dart about—the world is full of movement and activity. Although mobiles seem to relate directly to nature, it is nearly impossible to consider such sculptures without thinking of their inventor, Alexander Calder. Calder created countless mobiles during his lifetime, and seeing one of them is always a visual delight. In this activity, your students will be involved in learning about and constructing their own mobiles.*

1 Mobiles are quite popular and are available in many specialty stores and museum shops. Begin this activity by showing a mobile and holding a class discussion concerning it. Consider using some of the following questions in your discussion: What is a mobile, and what makes it move? What is meant by balance? Locate some books showing the works of Alexander Calder, and bring them to class to show the children.

2 Explain to the children that a mobile can be either "symmetrical" (the same on each side) or "asymmetrical" (different on each side). Draw some simple diagrams on the chalkboard to illustrate this fact:

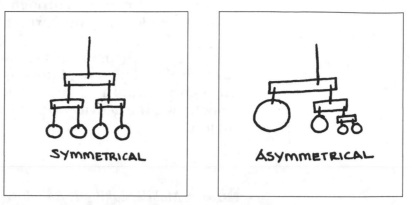

3 Distribute the newsprint and pencils, and ask each child to make a sketch for his/her own mobile. Point out to your students that mobiles may be based on different themes (such as birds or butterflies) or simply on interesting abstract shapes. It is up to each individual to decide what he or she wishes to do.

4 After the children have decided what they are going to do, each person can begin to work with the cardboard. Although cardboard is difficult to cut with school scissors, it can be done. Just encourage your students to "hang in there!" Once each student has completed cutting shapes, he/she should lay them on a table or desktop in the configuration he/she wishes.

5 Next, they should punch holes in each shape and attach either fishing line or thread. Advise your students that all strings must be well knotted. After they complete this step, the students can hold up their mobiles and see what happens. If the shapes get too tangled or the mobile doesn't seem to be balanced, the shapes may need to be adjusted (made larger or smaller).

6 When each child is satisfied with his/her mobile design, the shapes can be decorated using colored construction paper, tempera paint, or found objects. Point out to the students that objects, such as buttons, will add extra weight, which could change the balance of the mobile. Through "trial and error," the students will learn to work with this fact.

7 After all the mobiles are complete, arrange a display. The school library would be a fine spot for such a show. In addition, you may wish to conduct a poetry writing activity using the mobiles as the subject.

Notes: *Mobile making is an adventurous activity. A great deal of it involves experimentation and the idea of trying different shapes and designs. Although cardboard is a simple material, it enables students to gain insight into the characteristics of mobile construction.*

Once children get involved in making mobiles, they usually don't want to stop. However, sometimes in their haste to see what will happen, they don't tie the strings securely. Therefore, caution the students to do a good job in tying their shapes. In addition, since the project involves the idea of balance, you should be available for those children who may have problems getting their mobile off the ground.

A final word of caution about the overall size and length of the mobiles: Some of the students might create giant mobiles that may be too close to the floor when suspended. Although these are fun to look at, such creations might encourage tampering by other students since they are easily accessible. In light of this fact, it is a good idea to monitor the size of the mobiles and make sure that all shapes are out of reach when the creations are suspended.

Neighborhood Maps

Mapping Your Immediate World

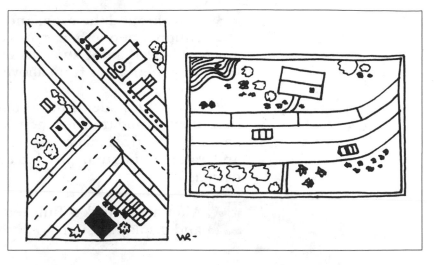

Purpose: *To learn to look at your neighborhood from a different perspective*

Materials:
Newsprint or manila paper (12" x 18"),
white drawing paper (12" x 18"),
pencils,
crayons,
markers,
watercolors,
brushes,
plastic cups,
water,
newspaper.

Description: *Every neighborhood has a distinct visual design and pattern. Particular buildings, houses, churches, temples, banks, stores, and schools make your neighborhood special and different from other places. In addition, trees, brooks, hills, and fields all help to make the place where you live unique.*

In this activity, you will be asking your students to map their immediate neighborhoods. To do so, they will be called upon to examine and think about where they live. Thus, a day or so prior to beginning the activity, ask each class member to take a good look at his/her neighborhood.

1 Launch the activity by bringing in some road maps and discussing their purpose. Why are maps important? What kinds of things do we learn from them? These are but a few of the questions that you can discuss with your class.

2 Next, ask the students to imagine that they are in helicopters flying over their neighborhoods. How would their houses or apartment buildings look from the air? How would other buildings look from above? What would the trees look like? How about cars? After discussing some of these ideas, distribute the newsprint or manila paper to the students. Ask each to make a rough sketch of his or her neighborhood, as if they were viewing it from above. The entire sketch should not include the whole town or city, but only a limited area (several blocks).

 Walk around the room and consult with the children about their map sketches. Try to resolve any problems that the students might have in visually recording their areas from above.

4 Once the students have completed their sketches, they should transfer their work to white drawing paper for the final maps. Colored markers, crayons, and watercolors can be used to enrich the final designs.

5 After all artwork is finished, hold a discussion and display session.

Notes: *This activity demands careful observation and thoughtful recall. Whenever I conduct it, I like to have the students imagine they are high up, as a bird or helicopter might be. Of course, children who live in high-rise apartment buildings may already get a bird's-eye view of their environment. Keep in mind that the view should not be from too high a vantage point since it would be very difficult to notice particular details of one's neighborhood.*

This activity, like many others in this book, is designed to encourage creative thinking and enhance "looking" skills. Although every child may not become an artist, I hope that each becomes a more sensitive and visually aware individual.

Ojo de Dios

A Yarn Charm

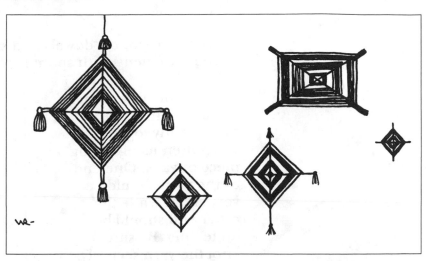

Purpose: *To understand the concept of a "talisman" and to develop skills in creating such an artwork*

Materials:
**Wooden dowels
(6" or 8" lengths),
coping saw,
a selection of
colored yarns,
scissors,
sandpaper.**

Description: *Throughout recorded time, the visual arts have been used to depict symbols for important religious and social institutions. In addition, artists have often played a vital role in creating charms to keep away evil and to bring good luck. Such charms are called "talismans."*

In Mexico and the southwest United States, one of the best-known talismans is the "Ojo de Dios" (Eye of God). The eye has often been used as a powerful symbol by many cultures around the world. In fact, if one looks closely at the back of a dollar bill, it is possible to find an eye. Such eyes are supposed to bring good fortune to their owners and keep away harm. The Indian peoples of Mexico and the Southwest create Ojos for this reason, and they also create them because they make very colorful decorations.

1 First, hold a class discussion on the importance of talismans, and show some examples of Ojo de Dios.

2 Next, explain, through simple diagrams or a demonstration, how to create an Ojo de Dios. Be certain to give all instructions before distributing any art materials:

a. Take two pre-cut dowels and sand the ends to prevent accidents with splinters.

b. Place the dowels next to one another, and tie them tightly together, in the center, using a long piece of yarn. One end of the yarn should be very short, while the other end should be quite long. Be sure to knot the yarn securely.

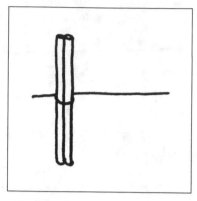

c. After tying the dowels together, take one dowel and place it in a cross or X position. Take the long piece of yarn and wrap it around the middle of the two dowels in an X pattern, in order to keep them in position.

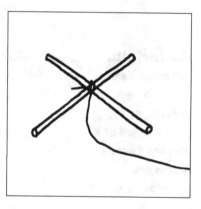

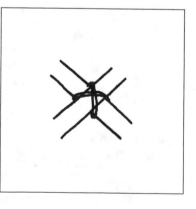

d. At this point, you are ready to begin wrapping the main body of yarn onto the dowels. To do this, hold the end of one dowel securely with your left hand, and following the diagram at the right, take the long piece of yarn and proceed to wrap it over and around each dowel. You will have to move your left hand to the next dowel while you pull the yarn tight with your right. (If you are left-handed, you'll have to reverse this process.) A diamond (eye) shape will begin to appear on the dowels.

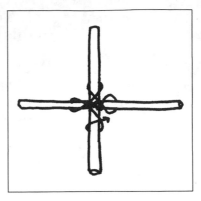

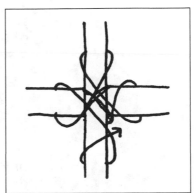

e. When you wish to change to a different color of yarn, simply knot the next color you want onto the end of the color you are using. When you reach the end of the dowels, double knot the yarn so that it doesn't slip out. Be sure to pull the yarn tightly as you do each row—your Ojo will look much sharper.

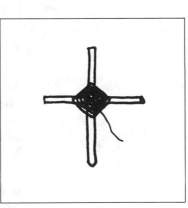

57

f. To create yarn tassels to attach to your Ojo, follow this procedure:

Cut a number of pieces of yarn the same length, and place them next to one another.

Tie a longer piece of yarn around the center of these pieces and knot it securely.

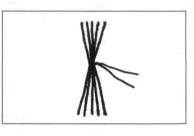

Brush all of the yarn pieces in the same direction, while holding the ends of the long piece of yarn at the center.

Tie a long piece of yarn about a third of the way down the yarn bunch, and knot it tightly. Even out the tassel by trimming the bottom with scissors. You are now ready to attach the tassel to your Ojo, using the long pieces of yarn from the center.

3 After you have explained the procedure to the students, distribute the materials and actual work can begin. It might help to repeat the above directions while everyone gets started at the same time. It is also important for you to pre-cut the dowels to either 6″ or 8″ lengths prior to the activity. Use a simple coping saw for this purpose. Be sure to tell the students that each Ojo has many color and design possibilities, and that no two Ojos should look alike!

Notes: *Creating Ojos is not that difficult, but it can be very time-consuming. Over the years, I have found that some students pick up the idea very quickly, while others take a bit longer. Ask those students who are moving along rapidly to help a friend who may be having trouble. In the initial session, you will repeat yourself many times, but it is well worth it. Once the students master the idea, they will be making Ojos for life. They're a bit like potato chips—if you try one, it's hard not to have another!*

Ojo de Dios make excellent holiday gifts and are a fine fund raiser for a school fair. Every year, my wife's fourth-grade students create a batch of Ojos, sell them at a class fair, and donate the money to a local charity. Such an idea can, indeed, bring good luck to many people in need.

59

Papier-Mâché Creatures

Fantastic Figures from Flour

Purpose: *To learn to design and construct three-dimensional forms from papier-mâché*

60

Materials:

**Newsprint or manila sketch paper,
pencils,
newspaper,
flour or wheat paste,
plastic cups,
water,
plastic bucket,
aluminum pie plates
or cardboard bowls,
small plastic
containers,
string,
masking tape,
corrugated
cardboard,
paper towels,
plastic drop-cloths
or old shower
curtain liners,
scissors,
tempera paints,
brushes,
glue,
found objects.**

Description: *Papier-mâché is a long-term activity that requires long-range planning. It is a project that is loads of fun but very messy. Therefore, if you are an individual who thrives on neatness and must always have things in meticulous order, you'd be wise to skip this activity.*

Before starting such a project, you and your class should decide whether you wish to create 1) smaller, individual creatures, where each child does his or her own, or 2) a single, larger class creature. Although the basic technique is the same, some aspects of the activity are different. In each case, however, make sure the children bring in plenty of old newspapers prior to starting the activity.

1 **Individual Creatures** Begin by explaining the process of papier-mâché to your students. You might point out that many things are made from this wonderful material. If you have any examples of objects made with papier-mâché, bring them to class and launch a discussion. Explain that papier-mâché paste is made by mixing flour or wheat paste with water and stirring it with your hands to achieve a consistency like very heavy cream. Small strips of cut or torn newspaper are then soaked in this mixture and applied to a skeleton or framework, like wet bandaids. However, the maker should be sure to wet the framework with the mixture before applying the strips. After each layer of papier-mâché has dried thoroughly, another layer can be added.

2 You may wish to set up a small demonstration, where the class watches as you mix and apply some papier-mâché. A skeleton or framework of a creature should first be made with rolled newspapers, string, and tape.

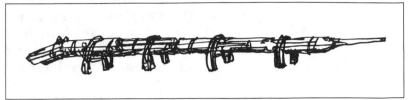

Since the process is a messy one, be sure to wear old clothes, take off all jewelry, roll up your sleeves, and keep all floor, desk, and table surfaces well covered. Although newspapers work well for this job, plastic drop-cloths or old shower curtain liners are best for large or long-term work.

3 Next, ask each child to choose a creature that they wish to make. This creature can be based on a real animal or it can be completely imaginary. Pass out some sketch paper, and have each student make a drawing of his/her creature. You should also encourage each child to imagine how the paper log skeleton should look.

4 After the students have completed their drawings, distribute old newspapers and have them begin rolling a batch of newspaper logs. Use masking tape to keep the logs from unrolling. (Be prepared to use lots of tape.)

5 Once the students have made a good supply of logs, they can begin to assemble the rough shapes of their creatures. They can tie the logs or tape them in bunches and then bend and fold them to form legs and wings. They can also add pieces of corrugated cardboard at this time. You should be available to give individual guidance and help as each child forms the framework of his/her creature. Keep in mind that this skeleton is only a frame and that with the addition of papier mâché, the skeleton will appear more detailed.

6 When all the skeletons are done, the class can begin the papier-mâché process. Make sure everyone is dressed appropriately, all jewelry is removed, sleeves are rolled up, and all floor, desk, and table surfaces are covered. Ask each child to tear up or cut a good supply of small newspaper strips. You should then mix the flour and water in a large bucket until the mixture is the consistency of very heavy cream. Next, give each child a pie plate or cardboard bowl and distribute the mixture to the class.

7 After everyone has received supplies, they can begin applying the paper strips to the skeletons. First, they should wet the skeleton using the mixture and then apply the wet paper strips. Try to watch that the skeletons don't get too wet. When the skeleton frames are completely covered, allow them to dry.

8 Clean-up will be time-consuming, since hands and arms will be somewhat difficult to clean. (This all helps to prove the amazing sticking power of simple flour and water!)

9 After a number of such sessions, the creatures will become stronger and more refined. Students can add a variety of textures and appendages by simply manipulating and balling up the wet paper strips and then letting them dry.

10 Once the papier-mâché work is finished and the creatures are completely dry, the painting and decoration can begin. Pipe cleaners, fake fur, yarn, ribbons, buttons, and plastic eyes are all great additions.

11 A final discussion and exhibition is, of course, an excellent conclusion to this activity.

1 **Class Creature** Once again, begin this activity with a discussion and explanation of the papier-mâché process. You may also wish to conduct a small demonstration.

2 Have the class decide on a single group project in which everyone will take part. This approach will involve a true "team effort."

3 After the children have agreed upon a single topic or theme, everyone will be asked to create a sketch of the creature. (You can take part also.) Encourage the students to think in terms of a simple newspaper skeleton as they do their sketches. Finally, the class should select one sketch to represent the entire group.

4 Next, have each child make a number of paper logs to be used in constructing the large skeletal framework. Working with groups of four or five children at a time, help supervise the building of this skeleton. A great deal of newspaper will be required, so keep the kids rolling. Needless to say, an abundant amount of tape and string will also be necessary.

63

5 After the large skeleton is completed, gather the children in small groups for the papier-mâché process. Cover a large table and the surrounding floor area with plastic drop-cloths or old shower curtain liners. Each group, dressed appropriately and free of jewelry, should be allowed to work, under your supervision, for about ten minutes. Then the first group will stop working and the next group will start, continuing the process. As with the individual creatures, you should do all the mixing and then distribute the mixture to the group. Students who are not working can be cleaning up.

6 Once the papier-mâché process has been completed and the creature is thoroughly dry, it can be painted and decorated. Keep in mind that several papier-mâché and decoration sessions will be needed.

7 Display the completed creature in the school library or front hallway. It will not only be visually intriguing, but it will also serve as a great example to inspire class pride.

Notes: *I have seen a veritable parade of papier-mâché animals: giant boa constrictors, bears of all kinds, horses, dogs, lions, leopards, strange "combination" animals, and creatures from other planets. Over the past five years, my wife's fourth-grade classes have been very interested in dinosaurs and have chosen to do a single large class creature each year. I have had the pleasure and joy of being involved in these long-term endeavors. The results have been a brontosaurus, stegosaurus, pteranodon, tyrannosaurus rex, and triceratops.*

My wife's classroom is always a source of great interest for the rest of the school, and her students enjoy conducting mini-tours to show off their latest creature. Some of the completed works have become permanent school library displays, while others, such as pteranodon, hang proudly from the ceiling of her classroom. Since each creature is approximately six feet long and three to four feet high, the greatest thrill for the children is the fact that they can create such a thing out of simple newspapers, flour, and water.

64

Paper Mosaics

Bits and Pieces

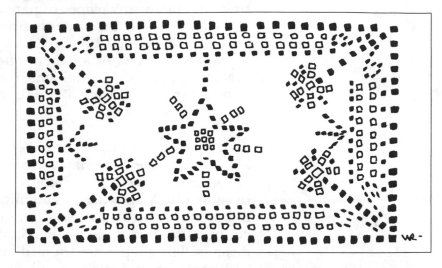

Purpose: *To create pictures and designs from tiny bits of paper*

Materials:
Newsprint or manila sketch paper,
pencils,
scrap colored construction paper,
assorted colored construction paper (12" x 18"),
large white or colored paper plates,
white glue,
scissors.

Description: *Mosaics are a very ancient form of art that have been used by many cultures throughout recorded history. Ancient Roman floor designs, Byzantine religious pictures, and Islamic floral patterns are but a few such examples. Perhaps the idea of using tiny bits of stone or glass to make a picture was inspired by a visit to the beach. Indeed, a walk along the shore, with all of its pebbles, bits of wood, and sea glass, is rather like walking through a large natural mosaic.*

In this activity, we will be concentrating on using bits of scrap colored construction paper rather than tiles or stones. However, the principle behind the activity is much the same.

1 Start the activity by showing and discussing some examples of mosaic art. You can enhance your discussion by bringing some books from the school library or by bringing a real mosaic from your own collection. Remember to tell the class that mosaic designs do not have to be realistic. They can also be abstract, decorative patterns. In fact, in our own times, we commonly see mosaics in floor and wall designs. Explain that mosaics are created by using bits of tile, stone, glass, or paper to make a picture or design. Usually these tiny pieces are glued to a surface with small spaces left between each piece. If tile, stone, or glass is used, these spaces are filled with concrete or grout.

2 Distribute sketching paper to the students, and ask each child to create a simple design or picture. It is a good idea to keep the design simple, since the many tiny pieces of paper will automatically add complexity. After students finish the sketches, each should select a 12″ x 18″ piece of colored construction paper or a paper plate to use as the base (background) for the final mosaic. They can then lightly transfer the sketch design to the construction paper or paper plate.

3 Next, the students should choose a number of scrap sheets in whatever colors they wish. These sheets can be cut or torn into tiny bits, which will become our "paper tiles." You might mention to the children that mosaic artists often use black or dark-colored tiles to outline the major shapes in their designs. The shapes are then filled with other colors. Although the students do not have to use this technique, such an idea does create strong contrast.

4 The paper tiles or bits are then glued into place following the design on the base sheet or plate. The gluing is time-consuming, since each tiny paper bit must be applied individually. However, the overall effect is well worth the effort!

5 After the children have completed their work, hold a discussion and sharing session as well as a follow-up mosaic exhibit.

Notes: *Nearly every classroom has an abundance of scrap paper of all kinds, colors, and descriptions. No doubt one of the favorite sayings of most teachers is, "Please don't waste the paper!" However, in their exuberance children often cut a small piece of paper from the center of a large one, creating a generous scrap. This activity is dedicated to the aesthetic use of all those great pieces of scrap paper. In addition, the exciting idea of using little bits of paper in a design is both intriguing and ecologically sound.*

A related activity could include asking your students to search their homes, school building, or local community for examples of mosaic art. Some communities have some excellent mosaics in religious structures, museums, and office buildings. The idea of encouraging the children to be on the lookout for such art will also help sharpen their awareness of their surroundings.

Paper Weaving

The Woven Way

Purpose: *To learn and understand the process of simple weaving*

Materials:
Colored construction paper (12" x 18") scissors, white glue.

Description: *Weaving can be a fascinating activity for older elementary school children. It is an activity that leads to a better understanding of an age-old process while providing the opportunity to create a multitude of varied designs and patterns.*

1 Launch this activity by discussing weaving and showing some woven products, including a variety of paper weavings. Explain to the children that weaving involves two components called the "warp" and the "weft." The "warp" is composed of the strands that run lengthwise in the loom, while the "weft" is made up of those strands that cross the warp.

2 Next, demonstrate the following steps before passing out any materials to the class. Since you will be using construction paper rather than fibers and looms, the "warp" section will consist of a single sheet of colored construction paper in which a pattern of cuts has been made. These cuts can best be accomplished by folding the paper down the center (widthwise) and then cutting from the fold toward the edges. Leave about an inch between each line cut, and be sure to stop cutting an inch or two from the edge.

This will leave a border around your warp sheet. Point out to the children that they can achieve a variety of different effects by being creative when cutting the lines.

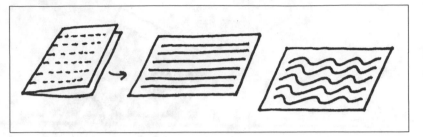

The "weft" is made by cutting long strips of 12" colored construction paper. Cut the paper widthwise, varying the width of the strips if you wish. Weave the weft strips into the warp paper by going over and under the warp strips. Make sure to place each weft strip snugly next to the last one and to alternate the over and under motion for each strip. In addition, glue the ends of the weft strips to the warp paper so that they won't slip out.

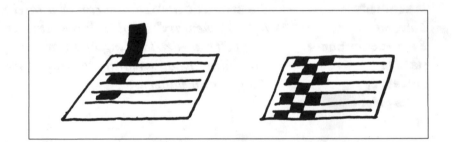

3 After demonstrating and explaining this information to the students, distribute the art materials and let them begin. It is a good idea to provide a wide variety of colored construction paper so that the children will have a nice choice. Be available to your students to help them resolve any difficulties that may arise.

4 After the children have finished the weaving, they may wish to cut small shapes (squares, circles, etc.) of other colors and glue them onto their designs to create extra interest.

5 Hold a final sharing session and exhibit at the conclusion of the activity.

Notes: *The tremendous variation in student works will no doubt amaze you. Although the process is quite simple, the idea of varying the paper colors, warp cuts, width of weft strips, and additional shapes will create lots of diversity. This is also one of those activities that is a bit like eating popcorn—namely, it is hard to stop at just one piece!*

I have often exhibited paper weavings on a single large wall, leaving no space between individual works. The result is a giant paper weaving, with a rather mysterious optical effect. If you have a large, empty display wall available, try this approach for some rave reviews!

69

Pointillism

Everyone Gets the Point

Purpose: *To experiment with and create designs using tiny dots of color*

70

Materials:
Newsprint and white drawing paper (9" x 12"), pencils, colored markers.

Description: *It is difficult to mention "pointillism" without thinking of the painter Georges Seurat. Seurat used tiny points of oil paint in creating his wonderful landscapes. Other artists have also been influenced by this technique, including Paul Klee and Victor Vasarely. In this activity, you will be introducing your class to the special technique known as "pointillism."*

1 Begin by explaining that this technique involves creating areas of color through the use of many tiny dots, with small spaces in between. Check the library for books showing artwork that employs this technique. If you have any art prints, bring them to class to enhance your discussion.

2 In order to keep this activity at a simplified level, use colored markers rather than paints. Explain to the students that each person will be creating a small artwork using pointillism. These works of art can be done in any style or on any subject that the students wish. You might also explain that by placing many marker dots of two colors next to each other, a third color will begin to become apparent (such as yellow and blue making green). This idea is often used in the printing process.

Pass out the materials to the children, and encourage them to experiment with this technique on newsprint paper. After they have decided on a subject, they can lightly sketch their idea using pencil on white drawing paper, filling in their designs with marker dots. Some students may wish to work on even smaller paper than a 9″ x 12″ piece, since the technique takes time.

4 When the students have finished, conclude the activity with a sharing session and exhibit.

Notes: *Small dots of color have lots of visual power. As the students get involved in using this technique, they should begin to appreciate this fact. Encourage your children to work carefully and take their time. Although they may wish to rush along, this activity definitely improves with additional time.*

Since pointillism has a definite optical effect, you might wish to couple it with the idea of creating optical illusions. By experimenting with this technique, the children will gain new insights into another method employed by some artists. Without question, as your students begin to experiment, I'm sure everyone will get the point!

Origami Puppets

Fantastic Folds

Purpose: *To create a puppet using Japanese paper folding*

72

Materials:
Colored construction paper (9" x 12"), paper scraps, assorted found objects, markers, scissors, white glue.

Description: *"Origami," the art of Japanese paper folding, can supply many hours of fun and enjoyment. Although you can make many things using a variety of folding techniques, in this activity we will concentrate on the creation of a very versatile paper puppet.*

1 Begin the activity by discussing Origami and showing a selection of completed puppets.

2 Before distributing any materials to your class, hold a demonstration of the basic method for folding the puppet:

Select a sheet of 9" x 12" colored construction paper and fold the paper in half, creating two 6" x 9" segments.

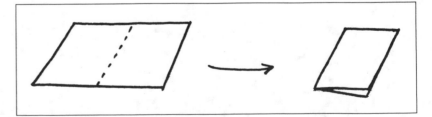

Fold the top 6″ x 9″ segment back to form two 3″ x 9″ segments.

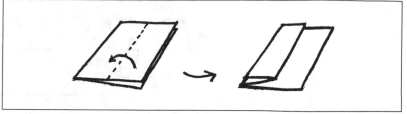

Next, turn the folded side over so that the plain 6″ x 9″ side is facing up toward you, and fold this segment back to form two 3″ x 9″ segments. Then unfold it again. This will create a foldline which will serve as a good reference line for the rest of the folding process.

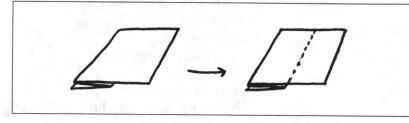

Keeping your paper in a vertical position, fold the top corners of the paper into a house-like shape. Be sure to line up the edges of each corner with the line you folded in the previous step. One side of the paper will be more difficult to fold than the other, since it is thicker.

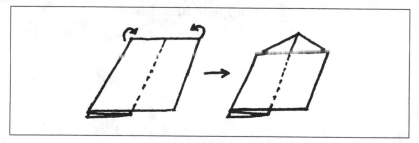

Turn your paper around, and fold the other two corners in the same way. Your paper should now resemble a marquise-like diamond shape.

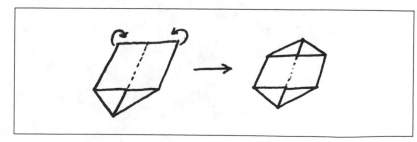

Next, turn this shape in a horizontal position, and fold it over to form a truncated pyramid.

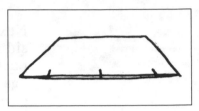

Holding this shape from the bottom, make three tiny cuts in the places indicated at the right. Each cut should be about ½″ in depth. Be certain to cut through the entire shape!

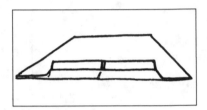

Fold the two resulting flaps back on the top of your shape in the following manner. They should look a bit like wing-flaps on an airplane.

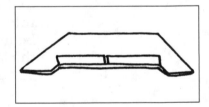

Next, turn the shape over, and fold back the two flaps on this side. The shape should now appear like this:

Gently open the shape by separating the two sides and putting pressure on each end. The mouth-like puppet shape that results should look like this:

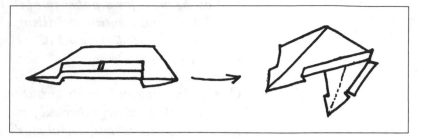

If all goes well, when you open and close the mouth, you should hear a clunking sound. This proves that your puppet head is healthy. Keep in mind that absolutely no glue is needed to create this basic form. It is now time to be creative with your puppet and decorate it however you wish. Glue eyes, fangs, hair, etc., onto your basic shape, giving it character and interest.

3 After you have completed your demonstration, pass out the paper and repeat the above steps with the entire class. Stress that each fold should be as accurate as possible. Take your time, and make sure the children understand each step.

4 After everyone has successfully completed the folding, they are ready to decorate. Students may wish to create bodies and hats for their puppets, as well as a multitude of facial features.

5 A series of puppet shows would be a fine culmination for this activity. This would enable each child to have a chance to introduce his/her creation in a unique way.

Notes: *This activity has always been a favorite with children. In fact, one of my elementary students introduced me to the basic fold over twenty years ago. By employing the fold as the basis for a paper puppet, my wife and I have entertained and creatively challenged thousands of children over the years. We have used it in classrooms, in airports, and at teacher workshops.*

One of the primary benefits of puppetry is that it can be related easily to many other subjects. Characters from reading, language arts, social studies, science, and, of course, imagination, can spring to life! I have had children make schools of fish, dragons, famous Americans, caricatures of their teachers, and a wonderful array of creative creatures. In addition to all these things, such an activity can bring confidence and excitement to overly shy children. Indeed, all these things and more can stem from a few fantastic folds.

76

Rod Puppets

Creating Storybook or Scrap Material Characters

Purpose: *To create original puppets inspired by ideas from storybooks and/or scrap materials*

Materials:
A wide variety of household items: paper or Styrofoam cups, plates, aluminum pans, drawing and construction paper, glue, scissors, markers, paper and fabric scraps, yarn, cardboard and/or lattice stripping (cut into 12" to 18" lengths).

Description: *Almost any object, whether two- or three-dimensional, can be attached to a flat stick or rod to create an exciting puppet. In this activity, students can make puppets using either the storybook or scrap material approach.*

The Storybook Method This approach encourages the students to develop their initial ideas from reading or listening to stories and to try to depict a storybook character in puppet form. Students can also use original stories and characters that they have invented. Each student should carefully note the various characteristics of his/her chosen character and attempt to illustrate the character through their artistic creation.

The Scrap Material Method Pie plates, milk cartons, pieces of cardboard, and Styrofoam are but a few of the many items that can prompt fascinating puppet creations. In this approach, the students may be motivated by an array of exciting materials and asked to construct a puppet based on these materials. Thus, the materials themselves should serve to stimulate and guide the students in their own imaginative directions.

After deciding which approach to use, the students might wish to make some sketches and then proceed to work. Make available great varieties of materials, arranged in plastic bins for easy access. The students should glue the different pieces of the puppet together before finally attaching the finished piece to the stick or rod. Flat sticks, such as long pieces of cardboard or lattice stripping (wood) are ideal, since they provide a flat rather than round surface for easy gluing.

When the puppets are completely glued and dry, the puppet shows can begin!

Notes: *One of the most amazing things about rod puppets is that nearly anything can be used to form a puppet. Imagine a group of puppets constructed from paper cups and plates. They might be called the "Picnic Puppets." Of course, kids always think of a thousand and one great ideas. In a recent class Batman appeared, along with a wide range of animal and monster puppets.*

This activity has a natural connection to other subject areas within the elementary curriculum. Language arts, in the form of script writing, and the illustration of famous historical characters from the social studies curriculum, are but a few of the things that spring to mind. By using a large desk or table for a stage, the students can kneel behind it and present their own puppet shows.

Sock Puppets

They Pack A Lot of Punch

Purpose: *To design and create a puppet from a single sock*

Materials:
*Old socks,
paper,
cardboard,
fabric scraps,
yarn,
plastic eyes,
buttons,
white glue,
scissors,
pencils,
markers.*

Description: *Sock puppets are not only fun and inventive, they also serve as a wonderful outlet for those single socks that sometimes appear in a washer or dryer. In addition, socks seem to be a natural when it comes to puppet designs. Their general shape just seems to invite the hand of a young puppeteer, and, by incorporating a few extra scraps, what once held a foot—now holds a character!*

1 Before beginning any work with your class, hold a sock drive to round up all those stray socks. Please stress that all the socks should be clean.

2 After collecting enough socks, you can present this activity to your class by showing a few completed sock puppets. If you like to use puppets, you might have them introduce themselves and speak about how they were made.

3 Explain to the students that each of us will be creating her/his own sock puppet. The children may either make a few sketches on paper of their ideas, or they can work directly on the socks. If they choose to work directly, have them hold off on the gluing until they are sure of their designs.

Distribute the materials to the students and let them begin to work. Be available to answer any questions as they arise. Students can create many types of heads and faces from their socks. If they wish to make a puppet with a hard mouth, have them cut a piece of cardboard, slightly smaller than the sock, in a bullet shape.

Place some white glue on one side of the cardboard and slide it into the sock. Press the sock into the glued side and let it dry. After drying, stuff cotton over the cardboard, and bunch it into a head shape. The cardboard can also be bent by hand to form a mouth.

5 Although students can glue noses, eyes, whiskers, etc., on the sock puppet, it is better to sew on most of these items, if at all possible. Bells are a fine addition, as well as yarn and fake fur. The use of sewing will guarantee that the puppets will last much longer.

6 When all the puppets are complete, hold a puppet introduction session and display.

Notes: *You can be certain that the kids will get a real kick out of sock puppets. Indeed, such puppets are great for creative storytelling, poetry, and social studies projects. They are also ideal for music and dance activities and show-and-tell games. In addition to these things, they provide an excellent vehicle for the non-verbal child to increase his/her communication skills.*

There is little question that sock puppets pack a lot of punch. I'm convinced that once you try this activity, you'll want to do it again and again.

Sandcasting

Impressions in the Sand

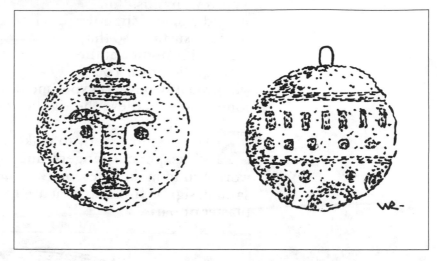

Purpose: *To design and cast relief sculptures using molds made from sand*

Materials:
Sand (approximately 2 buckets),
plaster of paris,
water (1 bucket),
1 empty bucket,
heavy waxed cardboard bowls or aluminum pie plates,
vegetable oil,
newspapers,
paper towels,
sponges,
tempera paints,
brushes,
string,
scissors,
plastic cups.

Description: *Sand is a curious material which abounds in certain parts of the country. If you happen to live near a large supply, you may wish to attempt sandcasting with your class. At the onset, this activity is a messy one; therefore, if you don't enjoy the gritty qualities of sand or the chalky residue of plaster, steer clear of this project.*

The whole idea of casting is a very ancient one, and, no doubt, the notion of using damp sand to construct molds is equally old. If you have been to the beach and scratched words or designs with a stick in the damp sand, or simply made footprints, you were halfway to a sandcasting!

Launch this activity by discussing the sandcasting process and showing a selection of already completed sandcastings. Do not give students any materials until they are completely clear about the process.

1 First, cover all work surfaces with newspaper. Then, select a heavy waxed cardboard bowl or aluminum pie plate, and coat the inside with a small amount of vegetable oil. Use a small piece of paper towel to spread the oil over all interior surfaces completely.

2 Next, place some damp sand into your bowl and firm it with your hands. You should create a slightly concave surface, so that the sand is higher at the sides of the bowl. You will probably have to experiment with the sand somewhat to achieve the right level of dampness.

3 You are now ready to make a design in the sand. Sticks, pencils, fingers, and many found objects work well to make lines, marks, and holes. When your sand design is finished, you are ready to use the plaster of paris.

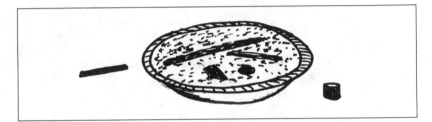

4 Plaster is a wonderful material, but since it can be messy, you should be the chief mixer and overseer. To mix the plaster, fill a large plastic bucket a little over halfway with water. Then carefully dump the dry plaster into the water in small quantities, until a small plaster island begins to form in the center of the bucket. After observing the plaster island for several moments to make sure that it does not sink into the water, you are ready to mix the plaster. Your hand and arm work best for this task. As you mix, make sure the mixture is smooth and lump-free. When it is thoroughly mixed to a heavy cream consistency, it is ready to be poured into the mold.

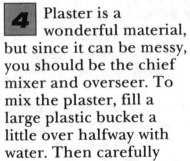

5 Using an empty milk carton or can, carefully fill the mold to the brim of the bowl or plate. Cut a small piece of string, and press the two ends into the wet plaster, creating a loop. This will enable you to exhibit your work better when it's dry.

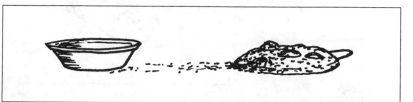

6 As the plaster dries it gets warm and solid. It is indeed an interesting chemical reaction. Leave the mold for several hours, and then carefully remove the casting from the bowl. The sandcasting can then be brushed off and rinsed in a bucket of water.

7 The results are always amazing, since some of the sand is forever embedded in the plaster surface. The raised portions of your design create a wonderful relief sculpture, which looks like something from King Neptune's house. The dry casting can be carefully painted with tempera or left unpainted.

8 After you have reviewed this process with your class, your students will be ready to go. Be sure the children are dressed appropriately, that all sleeves are rolled up, and that desks, tables, and the floor are well covered.

9 After the children have finished the activity, hold a discussion and display.

Notes: *Perhaps the most amazing quality of sandcastings is how old they look. No matter how often I've done this activity, the ancient results never cease to amaze me. The fascinating tactile quality of the sandy surface and the effects of small pebbles and mica chips embedded in the plaster is also quite interesting. You might have the children write stories about their sandcastings. They might pretend they are archaeologists who have recently discovered these perplexing finds!*

A school exhibit of these works is certainly a fine idea. I'm sure that many people will be puzzled as to how such artwork was created. The activity will certainly prove that there's plenty of mystery in the sands of time.

Sandpaper Works

The Magic of Marks

Purpose: *To encourage new insights into an aspect of Native American culture*

84

Materials:
Newsprint
(9" x 12"),
pencils,
sandpaper
(assorted
grits—
approximately
5" x 8"),
crayons and crayon
scraps.

Description: *The idea of this activity was directly inspired by Navajo sandpainting of the southwestern United States. Although we will not be creating sandpaintings in the traditional manner, the special qualities of sandpaper reflects, to some extent, a certain feeling of sandpainting. In addition, since sandpaper is a common material that is not difficult to locate, it has definite potential for such an activity.*

1 A discussion of sandpainting and its meaning in Navajo life should serve as an introduction to this activity. Discuss what the Southwest looks like in contrast to other parts of the United States. Visit your school and local library and obtain some books on Navajo art or Native American art of the Southwest. Be sure to show the children some examples of sandpaintings.

2 Since sandpaintings serve as magical works in Navajo art, they use special symbols and designs that relate directly to their culture. By looking at the examples, your students may be able to identify some of these symbols.

3 After your discussion, ask the class to draw their own designs, which relate to the sandpaintings you discussed. The newsprint sketch paper should be used for this purpose.

When the newsprint designs are complete, students can transfer their work to the sandpaper using the crayon and crayon scraps. They will find that the crayons will disappear quite rapidly, since they will be sanding the crayon with each stroke.

5 At the conclusion of the activity, hold a sharing session and exhibit.

Notes: *Although actual sandpaintings are temporary creations that are not meant to be kept, sandpaper works are more permanent. The special sparkle of the mica chips in the sandpaper give it a distinct glittering quality. By using crayon on this surface, you can achieve some very beautiful results. In addition, because sandpaper is available with a variety of surface grits from very coarse to very fine, I have found that the children enjoy experimenting with the varying textures.*

Since sandpaper is not usually linked to drawing, it can be thrilling for the students to do artwork on something generally associated with carpentry or woodworking. For that matter, I have heard some children comment that they have never seen sandpaper before. So, between introducing the children to an idea from a different culture, and having them work with a new material, you will be initiating some very special magic.

Scrolls

Picture Stories in a Roll

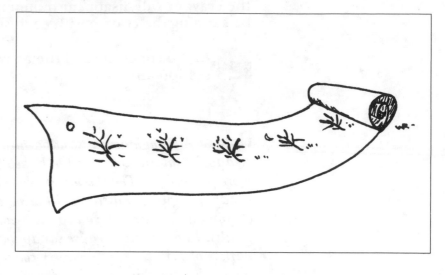

Purpose: *To depict a story using simple pictures on a long piece of paper*

Materials:
*Newsprint or manila sketch paper,
long sheets of manila or newsprint cut into 6" x 24" or 6" x 36" pieces,
pencils,
India ink (black and assorted colors),
watercolors,
brushes,
plastic cups,
water,
newspaper.*

Description: *The special beauty and charm of scroll painting is a distinctly Oriental one. Whether the subject is based on the world of nature or depicts the particular events of town life or religious festivals, scrolls relate stories, much like a length of movie film.*

Many books on Chinese and Japanese art are sure to include examples of scrolls. Therefore, you may wish to obtain some pictures or slides of scrolls before beginning this activity. You may also wish to create your own scroll to show your students.

1 Begin the activity by showing your class examples of scroll art. In so doing, launch a discussion on the unique characteristics of this art form. Some sample questions are: What is going on in the scrolls shown? How does the artist accomplish these things? Is the work simple or complicated?

2 After discussing scrolls and their purpose, ask the children to make up a simple story and devise illustrations for it on newsprint sketch paper. A flower blooming, a leaf falling, a dog walking, or a landscape at different seasons of the year are but a few possible ideas. Encourage the children to be imaginative, but also to keep their sketches simple.

3 After each child has decided on a theme and done the preliminary drawings, his/her work should be transformed to the long paper. The children may wish to re-sketch their designs lightly with pencil prior to using the ink or watercolors.

4 When the students begin to use the ink or paint, advise them to keep their work simple and direct. The paintings should have a spontaneous quality rather than a belabored one. If a child has an especially lengthy tale to relate, glue a few long sheets of paper together to form the scroll.

5 After the paintings are complete, the students should let them dry thoroughly. Then the scrolls should be rolled up carefully, so that the beginning pictures appear first as the scrolls are unrolled.

6 A showing and sharing session is a nice way to conclude this activity. In addition, a classroom, library, or hall display would certainly be a fine idea.

87

Notes: *The creation of scrolls affords the children an opportunity to think and work in a different realm. Since scrolls have a continuous quality, they present a different feeling than the separate pages of a book. It is very important to remind the students to keep their artwork simple and bold. In addition, advise them not to be overly concerned with errors, since these often add a human touch. For a very special effect, use rice paper if your budget permits.*

It might be fun to combine this activity with poetry writing. In order to do so, the children can contemplate their completed scrolls and write original poems about them. I would strongly recommend haiku poetry as a great corollary to this activity. If you decide to do this, there are many books available on the subject. Once again, the poems, like the scrolls, should be simple, clear, and spontaneous.

Still Life

An Object Lesson

Purpose: *To create drawings that reflect careful observation of objects in our world*

Materials:
Manila or white drawing paper (12" x 18"), pencils, ballpoint pens, markers.

Description: *Our lives are filled with a vast variety of objects. From vases to shaving cream cans, from detergent bottles to perfume bottles, from rocks to flowers, we're surrounded by a fantastic array of items with interesting shapes, colors, and textures. This activity utilizes a selection of objects as the basis for class work. The objects you choose and the way you present them to the children will have a definite effect on this art experience.*

1 The initial preparation for this activity should involve a kind of scavenger hunt for fascinating things that will provide good subject matter for still-life drawing. This object search can be handled in two distinct ways:

The Teacher Search: In this method, you become the chief investigator for objects. Check your home or apartment for things you believe might be interesting to your students. For example, children's toys, kitchen utensils, and sports equipment might be used, in addition to the usual bottles, cans, vases, and jars. Include pieces of fabric with a variety of patterns and designs. If you choose to collect all the items yourself, you can present the activity as a complete surprise to your class.

The Student Search: In this method, ask each of your students to bring in an interesting object or two from home. Advise them to choose something with a stimulating shape, color, or texture. Be sure to encourage them to use lots of imagination in their search.

2 Once the objects have been collected and brought to class, it is time to assemble your still life. Arrange the children's desks in a circle, and place the still-life on a table in the middle of the room. Be creative in how you set it up, and make it large and unusual. Somehow, seeing a batch of wonderful things all grouped together can excite the most reserved students.

3 Pass out the paper, pencils, and pens to the children and have them begin to draw. Encourage them to move around the circle in order to gain different viewpoints. In addition, have them vary their drawing material and try several drawings.

4 When the drawings are complete, hold a sharing session and follow-up exhibit.

89

Notes: *Artists have been involved in the creation of still-life works throughout the ages. Indeed, such an activity sharpens the eye to the amazing trappings that enliven our immediate environments. As a chronic "junk collector," I have, and continue to amass, a wide variety of objects. In fact, at this point in time, many friends are contributing curious items to my ever-growing collection. If you also enjoy collecting things, this activity is definitely for you!*

Sumi-E Painting

Beautiful Brushstrokes

Purpose: *To create ink drawings based on Japanese philosophy and technique*

90

Materials:
**Bamboo ink brushes
or watercolor
brushes (various
sizes),
water,
water cups,
ink stones,
ink sticks,
India ink,
watercolors,
paper towels,
manila, newsprint,
white drawing, or
rice paper
(12" x 18"),
newspaper.**

Description: *The Japanese perspective of nature, especially as reflected in Sumi-E painting, is quite different from our own. This technique is based on Zen Buddhist philosophy. The artist is encouraged to contemplate and finally become one with his/her work. As with any art, careful thought should be given to the idea. However, when it comes to actually creating the work, the Sumi-E painter should work rapidly and spontaneously.*

In this activity, we will begin to investigate Sumi-E painting. The primary idea, however, is to give your students a feeling of how another culture views and creates a particular kind of art.

1 Before presenting any information to your class, you should begin gathering books, prints, and art materials dealing with the topic. Look under "Sumi-E painting" or "Japanese art" in libraries, museum shops, or Oriental variety stores. Prints or book illustrations of such art should not be difficult to locate.

The special ink stones, ink sticks, and bamboo brushes used in this art may be more difficult to find. Although Oriental variety shops sometimes stock these items, a good art supply shop should be able to help. As with any art activity, if you have never tried Sumi-E painting, you should experiment on your own before starting to work with your class.

2 Your presentation to the class should reflect the feeling of a different culture. Discuss Japanese ink painting and calligraphy. How does such writing differ from our own? Show pictures and books on Sumi-E painting, and be sure to convey the idea that the artist should think carefully about his/her subject and then work rapidly. You might also wish to play some Japanese music to create a special mood.

3 Next, conduct a demonstration of how the ink used in this form of painting is made. Ask the students to gather around you, and allow them to participate in the process. Explain that even the creation of the ink from solid to liquid form is a kind of special ritual. To grind the ink:

Pour a small amount of water into the well of the ink stone.

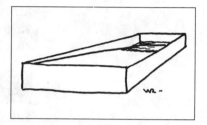

Hold the ink stick firmly in your hand, between your thumb and index finger, and rub the stick back and forth along the slanted surface of the ink stone. Be sure to wet the ink stick with each motion by letting it come in contact with the water. As the stick is moved across the wet stone, the liquid ink begins to form and collect in the well of the stone.

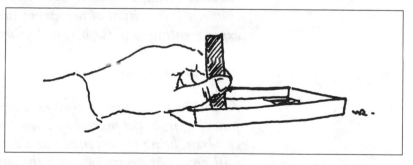

After grinding the ink for a short time, you can test out how dark it is by dipping your brush into the mixture and trying a few sample strokes on a piece of newsprint. The basic ink should be rich and black.

4 If you are lucky enough to have several ink stones and ink sticks, you can supervise a number of groups grinding ink at the same time. Pour finished ink into plastic cups for later distribution. If you don't have enough ink stones and sticks, you can supplement your supply with India ink. Be certain, however, that each student gets a chance to experience the process of grinding ink.

5 When the ink is ready, pass it out to the children, along with some brushes, a small cup of water, drawing paper, and paper towels. Encourage each child to experiment with his/her brushes on newsprint or manila. Allow them to discover that by holding and moving the brush in different ways, they can create a variety of effects. Point out that by adding varying amounts of water to the ink, they can make different values or shades. If the brushes get too wet, students can blot them on the paper towels.

6 When the students have developed some confidence in using the ink and brush, they can select a theme and attempt a complete ink painting. Be sure to advise them to work simply and rapidly.

7 As a culminating event, hold a sharing session and exhibit at the conclusion of the activity.

Notes: *Perhaps the most exciting part of this activity for children is the ritual of preparing the ink and the fun of experimenting with the brush. I believe that activities such as this one give students a wonderful opportunity to learn about different ways of thinking and working in art.*

As with many of these activities, the major stress in Sumi-E painting is on the process and not the product. However, children, being the inventive and creative people they are, will no doubt amaze you with the many things they produce. Ink paintings with both sensitivity and humor will probably appear, to the delight of both you and your class!

Totem Poles

Sacred Sculptures

Purpose: *To design and construct a large totem using contemporary materials*

Description: *Totem poles are always an adventure for the eye and mind. The faces of birds, animals, and people carved into the wood of a large log create an impression of power and mystery. In this activity, your class will be building a few large cardboard box totems.*

Materials:

Newsprint (9" x 12"), pencils, cardboard boxes (not too large), markers, colored construction paper, tempera paints, brushes, newspapers, paper towels, plastic cups, glue, string, picture wire, wire cutters and pliers, found objects.

1 Before introducing the activity, collect a good supply of empty cardboard boxes. Shoe boxes are especially handy for this project. When you are ready to begin, show some pictures of actual totem poles, and discuss why the Indians of the Northwest Coast created them. Explain that although these artists use logs because they are plentiful in their environment, we will be using cardboard boxes, which are plentiful in ours.

2 Give each child a sheet of 9" x 12" newsprint to create some sketches of a face or group of faces. It is important to keep in mind that the boxes will have four visible sides, which the students must deal with. The children can create a different design on each side of the box or create all parts of a three-dimensional head. These designs can represent humans, birds, or animals, or they can be completely imaginary.

After the children have completed their sketches, give each child a cardboard box, and let them transfer their sketch designs to the box using pencil.

 Once the designs have been drawn, the students are ready to use marker, cut paper, and tempera paint. Be sure the children are dressed appropriately and that all table and/or desk tops are covered with newspaper.

5 When all the boxes are completely dry, stack them on top of one another in totem pole fashion. Students should form small groups for this section of the activity, with four or five children in each group. Use white glue to hold the boxes together, or punch two holes at the bottom and top of each box and insert string or wire. The box at the base of the pole should contain some weight, such as a heavy stone or brick. This will keep the poles steady and prevent toppling. As a final touch, add cardboard or construction paper wings and arms and glue found objects, such as feathers and buttons, to the poles.

6 Hold a final discussion session at the conclusion of the activity, followed by a totem pole exhibit.

Notes: *This activity can be easily connected to the study of Native American art, especially that of the Indian tribes of the northwestern United States and Canada. In addition to doing artwork, ask the children to do some research on the meaning of totem poles.*

At the Museum of Natural History in New York City, there is a wonderful room filled with many majestic examples of Northwest totems. The room is dim and rather mysterious. As a follow-up to this activity, you might wish to turn your classroom into such an exhibit hall and invite the rest of the school. Position your totems around the room, interspersed with fact sheets and information; then, dim the lights and invite some visitors!

Part Three

Adventures in Design

The domain of imagination is central to this portion of the book. It is a sphere filled with infinite potential and promise. It is a place where new ideas and images spring to life and take visual form. These ideas may be based upon previous experiences, things never actually experienced, or a combination of both.

The world of our own imagination challenges each of us to build creative works that are vitally connected to our special individualism. In this section, we will proceed down pathways of the senses and create new languages of vision. We will build monsters, fly into the skies, and explore under the seas. We will experiment with materials, construct machines that do nothing, and write and illustrate original stories.

The many diverse ideas presented here can be used as a springboard to new discoveries. The only criteria for success is that each person makes an honest attempt to learn from him/herself and creates art based upon that learning. Keeping these things in mind, let us all join in this exciting and stimulating expedition!

Book Jackets

Judging a Book by Its Cover

Purpose: *To design and illustrate a book jacket with exciting visual appeal*

Materials:
*Newsprint,
manila and white
drawing paper
(6" x 9"),
pencils,
markers,
watercolors,
brushes,
plastic cups,
water,
newspaper.*

Description: *There can be little doubt that the printed word has changed the world. However, before we even start to read a book, we are often attracted to it by its cover illustration. Generally, works of fiction and children's storybooks have the most imaginative book jackets. These covers are especially designed to sell the book through their unique artwork. In this activity, the students will pretend they are authors and/or illustrators, whose assignment involves creating stimulating cover designs that will help sell their books.*

1 Begin this activity by presenting a number of book jackets to the class and launching a discussion on why such art is important in the publishing field.

2 Ask each child to pretend he or she is an author/illustrator who must create a book jacket cover design for his/her new book. The book may either be imaginary or already in existence.

3 Once the children have decided on their books, they can begin sketching their ideas on newsprint or manila paper. Encourage them to make a few preliminary drawings before selecting a final design.

4 The final designs can then be selected and carefully transferred to the white drawing paper using pencil. Students can color the designs with markers and watercolors.

5 When all the students have completed their book jackets, hold a show-and-tell session with your class. A follow-up exhibit in the school library would be a wonderful culminating event for this activity.

Notes: *Since art has many facets and connections, this activity is a fine way to get children to see the link between art and business. Although in theory books should not be judged by their covers, this is often not the case in the publishing industry.*

Encourage the children to be creative and imaginative. I have confidence that they will think of plenty of great ideas filled with humor and interest. Indeed, perhaps such an activity will spark a future author or illustrator!

Changing Portraits

Features with a Flip

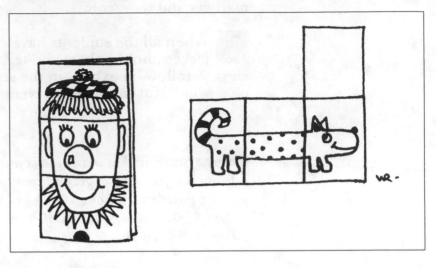

Purpose: *To design a moveable, multi-imaged artwork from a single sheet of paper*

Materials:
*Newsprint,
white drawing paper
(12" x 18"),
scissors,
crayons,
markers,
pencils.*

Description: *The mystery and excitement of "change" forms the basis for this activity. By folding and cutting several paper flaps, the design potential of one piece of paper becomes enormous.*

1 Launch this activity by showing several examples of "Changing Portraits." You might also locate a few children's books done in this style and show them to your class.

2 Hold a discussion with your students on how the creation of multiple images creates an exciting design. Then explain how to cut the paper, which will set the stage for the rest of the activity:

Take a single sheet of 12" x 18" white drawing paper and fold it carefully into thirds:

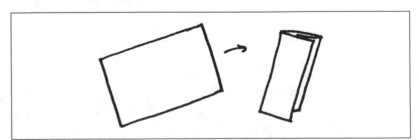

Next, cut the uppermost flap into three equal segments:

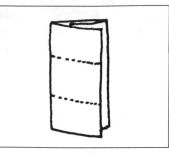

Using your pencil, mark off two lines on the next flap, using the top cuts as a guide. Then, unfold the top flap, and cut these segments as you did above.

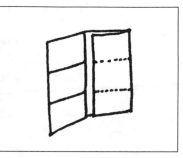

When your paper is unfolded, it should look like the figure below. Do not do any cutting in the central section of your paper.

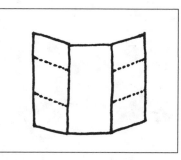

You are now ready to decorate each flap with your own designs.

 Before distributing the white drawing paper to the students, have them make some preliminary sketches of their ideas on newsprint. After they have selected their favorite idea, pass out the white drawing paper and have them cut and draw their design.

4 Some students will start their drawings on the uncut middle section, while others will begin on the first flap. Keep in mind that there is no one way to begin. In addition, remember that the number of segments cut on each flap can also be varied. The final designs should be enhanced using colored markers and crayons.

5 When the works have been completed, hold a sharing session and exhibit.

Notes: *Although I have titled this activity "Changing Portraits," the subject matter need not be limited to people or faces. Children have created wonderful cars and motorized vehicles using this method. They have also made fantastic houses, space ships, and airplanes, plus a wide range of wild and unusual animals and monsters.*

Once the kids realize the enormous potential of having a series of moveable flaps on their paper, they will simply take off with the idea! The really amazing thing is that such a project requires only a single sheet of paper and very few materials. I would strongly recommend it for those schools that are very low on art supplies. You can be certain that all the children will enjoy getting involved in this fun-filled activity.

100

Clay Works

Art from Earth

Purpose: *Learning to use some selected methods in working with clay*

Materials:
Plasticine, newsprint (12" x 18"), plastic picnic utensils, found objects.

Description: *Clay is a truly remarkable substance that has served as a major artistic medium throughout the ages. One of the chief indicators of past cultures is their clay pottery and sculpture that has survived to the present day. Although there are many kinds of clay, in this activity we will be using plasticine.*

Plasticine has many of the same qualities as regular earthenware clay. However, due to an oil-like additive, it cannot be fired. Rather, it can be left to dry to a leather-hard state, which can be stored for a long period of time. The real advantage of plasticine is that it can be re-used again and again. If you rework the hardened material in your hands for a short time, it will become softer and more pliable.

In this activity, we will be focusing on three classic methods of clay work. These methods are the Pinch Method, the Coil Method, and the Slab Method.

1 Begin the activity by discussing the three methods mentioned above. You may wish to show some diagrams or use the chalkboard to illustrate these methods. In addition, you might have the class gather around you for a short demonstration. Finished pieces of pottery or sculpture which show these methods are, of course, a fine addition to this portion of the activity.

The Pinch Method: This technique is probably the simplest of all clay working techniques. Starting with a lump of plasticine, the artist merely "pinches" his/her clay into the desired shape. Pinch pots and pinch sculptures can be found throughout the world.

The Coil Method: Children often refer to this method as "making snakes." The idea is to roll out thin "coils" of plasticine and then use these coils to construct a pot or sculpture. Coil pottery can be built to great heights and is often smoothed out so that the viewer may be unaware of how it was constructed.

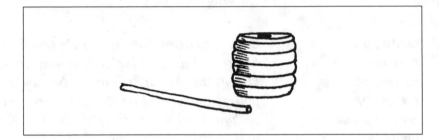

The Slab Method: In this method, the plasticine is flattened, like a piece of pie crust or dough. The flattened pieces are usually cut or smoothed into square or rectangular shapes. These shapes are then pressed and smoothed together to create a three-dimensional form.

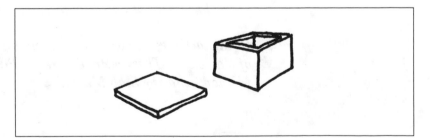

2 After introducing the students to the three methods, distribute the materials to the class and let them begin working. Be sure that each child places a piece of newsprint on his/her desk before using the plasticine in order to simplify clean-up. Encourage the children to try all three methods you discussed. In addition, let them experiment with various surface treatments by using the plastic picnic utensils and found objects.

3 Once the children have completed their sculpture or pottery, hold a sharing session. If you have a showcase, hold a claywork exhibit.

Notes: *Plasticine is one of those materials that people either like or dislike. Since it is a tactile material, you must get your hands dirty. Some people, both children and adults, seem to have an aversion to doing this. If a few of the students in your class seem reluctant to experiment with plasticine, encourage them to give it a try.*

There is no question that clay is a material that demands direct involvement. However, often the individual who is at first timid about using clay becomes an avid potter or sculptor, so be patient and supportive. Although the chief benefit of this activity is in the "process," the children will no doubt create some exciting "products." Remember, however, that the goal of the activity is to learn some methods that can be used to work with this wonderful material.

103

Compass Designs

Magic Circles

Purpose: *To create experimental designs using a compass*

104

Materials:
White drawing paper (12" x 18"), compasses, rulers, pencils, crayons, markers.

Description: *Over the years, the special characteristics of circles have intrigued human beings. A circle is truly a shape of magic. It has no beginning, and it has no end—it's continuous. In this activity, we will explore the artistic potential of circles.*

1 Begin this activity by discussing some of the many circular shapes we encounter in our world. Ask the children what circular objects they see around the classroom. What other objects, based on the circle, do they notice either at home or in the community? Make a list of these objects on the chalkboard.

2 Although circles can be drawn freehand, ask the class what instrument can be used to create circles. Explain how a compass works, and caution the children about its dangers.

3 Next, show your students a variety of designs made by using a compass, and explain to them that this will be the theme for the activity. Stress the fact that each person should try to experiment with his/her compass and create as many varied designs as possible. The designs should include a wide variety of sizes and patterns. The circles can overlap, be separate from one another, or continue off the paper, if the students wish.

Distribute the supplies to the children and let them begin work. Some students may have an initial problem learning to use a compass, so be available for individual guidance.

5 Once the students have completed their designs, they can color them in using crayons and markers.

6 A sharing session and exhibit should be the culminating event.

Notes: *Circles are everywhere—from new designs in hubcaps and steering wheels to the fantastic multicolored wonders of stained glass windows. By developing their skills in using the compass, the children will be well on their way to creating some exciting circular designs.*

Although each completed artwork is fine to display in its own right, you may wish to formulate a large, continuous exhibit using all the works together. To do this, cover a large wall with the students' work without leaving space between each design. Carefully line up the edges of each piece next to another one and affix them to the wall. The result will be a circular adventure, which can stretch across a large space. This is just another way to demonstrate the magic of circles!

Drawing to Music

A Visual "Note"

Purpose: *To let the varied characteristics of musical selections stimulate visual forms*

Materials:
Assorted records and cassette tapes, record player, cassette tape recorder, white drawing paper (12" x 18"), crayons, markers.

Description: *Music fills a tremendous need in our lives. It helps lull us to sleep and stimulates us to wake. It calms us, excites us, makes us happy and sad. All of us have favorite songs, melodies, and musical instruments. In addition to the joys of listening to music, many people are skilled in creating it. In this activity, you will be presenting some musical selections to your class and encouraging them to react in a visual way.*

1 Prepare for the activity by locating the various pieces of music you wish to use. Be ingenious in your search, and attempt to present both familiar and unfamiliar selections. I have found it effective to choose six or seven records or tapes and then make a single cassette recording that includes segments of each selection. The total length of the tape should be about twenty minutes.

2 After your tape or records are ready, you can present the material to your class. Before passing out the paper, crayons, and markers, briefly explain the theme of the activity to the children. It is a good idea to tell them that their visual reaction to the music can be in any style they wish. Designs can range from abstract linear patterns to realistic forms. Be sure to encourage the students to listen carefully to the music and try to make their visual marks match the particular piece.

3 Distribute two sheets of paper, crayons, and markers to each child. Then play your tape or records and let the students begin to work. You may wish to work along with the class or walk around the room as the music plays.

4 After listening to all the musical selections, hold a sharing session. As a follow-up, ask the children to write a story about the artwork they created, and, of course, hold an art exhibit.

Notes: *This activity is an excellent way to get children to see the relationship between one sense and another. Many artists have created visual works with musical connections. Marc Chagall, Paul Klee, and Pablo Picasso are a few such artists. In addition, I have found that this is a wonderful method of introducing children to forms of music that they may never have heard before.*

Since many children play musical instruments, you may wish to follow up this activity by inviting some of your class musicians to perform a few selections. The class could also draw while the musicians play. The entire activity should stimulate "noteworthy" interest and excitement.

107

Drawing from Odors

Scent-Stimulated Signs

Purpose: *To create artwork that has been motivated by a variety of scents*

108

Materials:
Jars and/or containers of assorted scents, white drawing paper (12" x 18"), crayons, markers.

Description: *The entire environment in which we live is packed with an amazing amount of aromas. Our sense of smell is one of our basic senses, and, in this activity, students will use that sense to aid them in creating visual designs and pictures.*

1 Before introducing the activity to your class, collect a wide variety of different scents to present to the children. The kitchen spice shelf is a fine place to begin. You may wish, however, to put a small amount of each spice you select in an unlabelled jar so the class will not see its name. Perfumes, soaps, coffee, and tea are also good products to use. When all the scents are ready, place the jars or containers in a box and bring them to school.

2 Explain to the children that you will be circulating a number of different scents. Each child should smell each sample and then pass it to the next person.

3 Next, pass out the paper, crayons, and markers, and ask each student to select the scent they liked the most and make a drawing or design of what it suggests. The artwork can be in any style the individual wishes, from abstract patterns and shapes to very realistic representations.

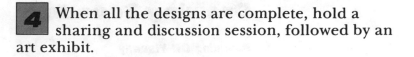 When all the designs are complete, hold a sharing and discussion session, followed by an art exhibit.

Notes: *My wife is a wonderful baker, and our house is usually filled with the fantastic scents of baking bread, pies, or cookies. Working with scents is exceptionally interesting and fun. The suggestive power of a simple odor is indeed phenomenal and can stimulate all kinds of connections in the visual arts. Colorful scenes of exotic islands and deserts, wonderful plants, and rhythmic linear patterns often result.*

During your sharing session, you may wish to hold a "guessing game," where the children attempt to figure out which scent motivated which drawing. You might also want to try a variation of this idea by conducting a similar activity with the sense of taste. Bring in some homebaked goods or a variety of fruits. Then, after enjoying a pleasant snack, ask the children to create visual works based on the experience. Both activities help us to appreciate our sensory powers.

Drawing Sounds

Purpose: *To create visual works that have been motivated by various sounds*

110

Materials:
Cassette tape recorder and tapes, white drawing paper (12" x 18"), crayons, markers.

Description: *As we listen to the world around us, many sounds evoke particular thoughts and images. The wail of a train whistle, the howling of a strong wind, and the perking of a coffee pot are but a few of these. In this activity, you will be collecting a group of sounds and using them to sensitize and inspire your students to create artwork.*

1 Before launching this activity with your class, you need to get a cassette tape recorder, with good batteries, and a few blank tapes. Then start to collect sounds. This job is both fascinating and fun, since it will eventually set the stage for your students' artwork. What sounds do you especially notice? What sounds do you think the students will enjoy or be challenged by? These are but two questions that you may wish to ask yourself on this quest. Record each sound for about thirty seconds, and then move on to another one. You might also create sounds by banging pots with spoons, crumpling paper, etc. Music can also be used between other sounds. Try to be imaginative and creative in formulating your tape.

2 After you have finished making your sound tape, you are ready to introduce it to the children. Briefly explain that you will soon be playing a tape recording of a variety of sounds to the class. As the students listen to each sound, their mission will be to make a drawing about it. Each child should be given a sheet of paper and asked to group all the sounds he/she hears on that sheet. The drawings can be in any style or format the students wish.

3 Distribute the drawing paper, crayons, and markers to the class and start the tape. Encourage the children to listen carefully and to use their imaginations.

4 When the tape is over, the students can share and discuss their works. You might also review the different sounds you played and ask the class to identify them. A sound drawing exhibit should follow this discussion.

Notes: *Drawing sounds is a stimulating and thought-provoking activity. It challenges the children to become more careful listeners, while, at the same time, they learn to associate and relate one sense to another. Although the drawings may be exciting, the real meaning of this activity is in the doing.*

In addition, the creation of the motivational sound tape should be an interesting challenge. Over the years, I have recorded trains leaving stations, the wind off the bay, keys jingling, kettles bubbling, flutes blowing, paper tearing, and many more. All of these things can help inspire students to sound off visually.

111

Dream Houses

Every Home Should Be a Castle

Purpose: *To design an imaginary house that reflects the individual's personal tastes*

Materials:
*Manila and white
drawing paper
(12" x 18"),
pencils,
rulers,
compasses,
colored pencils,
markers,
watercolors,
brushes,
plastic cups,
water,
newspaper.*

Description: *If you could design and build the house of your dreams, what would it look like? Where would it be located? What style would it be, and what materials would be used to construct it? These are but a few of the questions to consider when you begin this activity. The crucial thing to remember is that each student's dream house should reflect his/her own personal tastes.*

1 A good way to start this lesson is to ask your class questions like those listed above. Then hold a brief discussion centered around the students' responses.

2 Next, show some book illustrations or photographs of fascinating houses in a variety of styles. You can obtain some fine books on architecture at the library. You might also look up such well-known architects as Frank Lloyd Wright, Le Corbusier, and Ludwig Mies van der Rohe.

3 After this introduction, ask your students to think carefully about the "dream house" they would like to own. Pass out the 12" x 18" manila paper, pencils, rulers, and compasses, and have each child begin making sketches of his/her ideal house.

Once the children have made a number of sketches, ask them to select their favorite and transfer it to the 12" x 18" white drawing paper. They should use pencil for their initial drawing and add marker and watercolor later.

5 When the final drawings are finished, hold a sharing session and architectural exhibit.

Notes: *Everyone likes different things, and house designs are no exception. It is amazing how elementary students have distinct preferences and interests when it comes to designing their "dream houses." In doing this activity, remind the children that they are not limited by money or materials. After all, this is going to be their ideal house.*

"Dream Houses" challenge the individual child to develop ideas that conform to his/her own unique tastes. I believe that this idea is at the core of the whole activity, for it encourages each student to listen to and value his/her own interests and concerns and then base a creation upon them. Who knows what future architects may be inspired by such a pursuit!

Finger Painting

Hands Full of Color

Purpose: *To experience the tactile joy of working with color in a direct manner*

Materials:
Finger paint (various colors), finger painting paper (large sheets), tongue depressors, small sponges or sponge pieces, plastic pail, water, newspaper.

Description: *Although finger paint is generally associated with younger children, it offers a marvelous sensory opportunity for people of all ages. The pleasure and exhilaration that accompanies such an experience should not be missed. Needless to say, finger painting can be messy, and it requires advanced attitudinal preparation on the part of the teacher. If the desk or table tops in your classroom are formica, you may wish to sponge them off at the conclusion of your activity (rather than covering them with newspaper). Be sure that the students are dressed appropriately on the day of the activity and that all jewelry is removed and all sleeves are rolled up.*

1 Start the activity by distributing finger painting paper and wet sponges to your students. The shiny side of the paper should be facing up, and each student should coat his/her paper with water from the sponges.

2 You are now ready to pass out the finger paints. Using the tongue depressors, give a scoop of color to each child. Allow the students to pick and choose their colors.

3 After you have distributed all the colors, let the fun begin! Encourage your class to experiment with different finger and hand motions. Let them also mix the colors and do a number of paintings.

4 When the works are completely dry and the room is cleaned up, hold a sharing session followed by a finger-painting exhibit.

Notes: *Finger painting is a direct experience that definitely requires getting your hands dirty. As with many art activities in this category, the process is more significant than the product. The sense of freedom and fun that such an activity fosters will often outweigh the final results.*

If you are working with children who have special learning needs, I would highly recommend such an activity. However, I would suggest that instant pudding be used as a substitute for finger paint. Although finger paint should be non-toxic, there is often a higher risk that such a student population may attempt to taste the paint.

Finger painting starts with getting your hands full of color and ends by giving you a heart full of joy!

115

Flicker Planes

A Flighty Thing

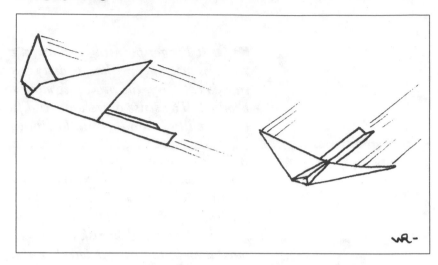

Purpose: *To create an aerodynamic design as a basis for further experimentation*

Materials:
Standard white duplicating paper (8½" x 11"), scissors, pencils, markers.

Description: *People have always had a desire to fly. Many ancient myths, such as the story of Icarus, refer to the idea of human beings attempting to soar like the birds. Through exceptional curiosity and persistence in the fields of science and art, people have been able to do just that.*

In this activity, we will be learning and experimenting with a special paper airplane design called "The Flicker," which was first shown to me by my late friend George Schulman. An inquisitive engineer, he took delight in demonstrating this special design to all who were interested. I, in turn, have happily shown many children how to make "The Flicker."

1 Before doing this activity with your class, it is a good idea to practice making a number of planes so that you fully understand the process.

Start by taking a piece of 8½" x 11" paper and folding it into the shape of a triangle by taking one corner and pulling it over to look like this:

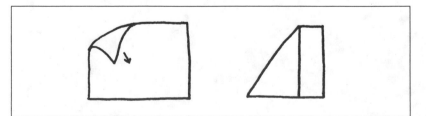

Using your scissors, cut off the extra rectangle of paper. Be sure to save this piece, since you will need it later.

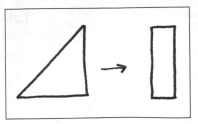

Next, open up the triangular shape to form a square.

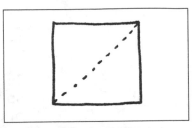

Fold this square into a triangular shape the other way, as shown below, and open it up again.

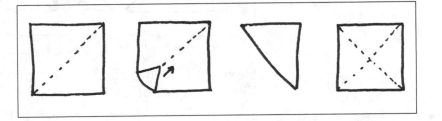

Your square should now look like this:

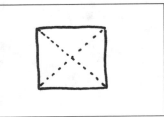

Turn the square over so that the two fold lines are facing the desk top, and fold the paper in half, forming a rectangular shape.

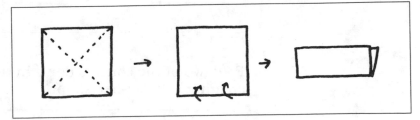

Then, once again, unfold the paper. Your shape should now appear a bit raised and three-dimensional.

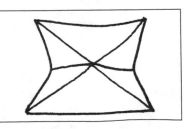

Taking this shape, gently press in on either side, along the line you last folded, to form a triangular shape.

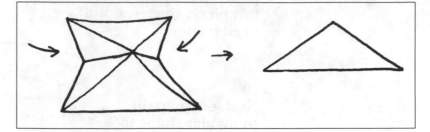

Since this shape is composed of two triangles, take the top triangle, which is facing up, and fold it in the following manner.

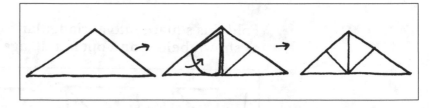

Next, fold the two small triangles over so that they look like the figure below.

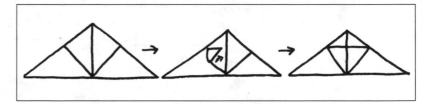

Now, take your leftover rectangular piece, fold it in half the long way, and unfold it.

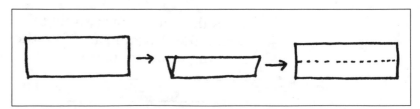

Fold two of the corners down in the following fashion, creating a rocket-like shape.

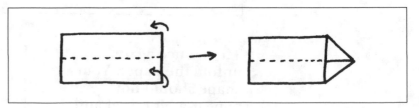

Insert this rocket-like shape into the triangular wing you created with the largest piece of paper. Be sure to press the rocket shape all the way to the front of the wing shape.

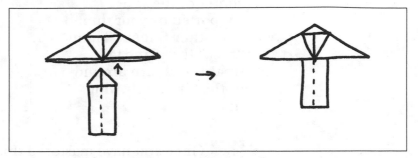

Now, solidly fold down the topmost nose of the wing so that it appears like the figure below.

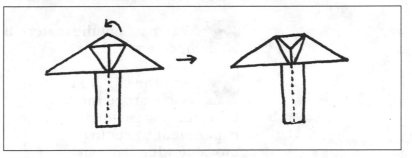

Finally, fold the wing and tail sections in half, and unfold them in the following manner.

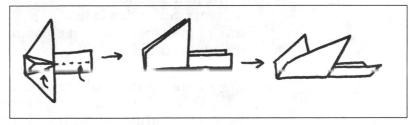

To fly the flicker, hold the front of the plane toward you, and place your index finger in the center of the wing, supported by your thumb and other fingers. Then "flick" the plane tail first! It will turn around in the air and fly wing first.

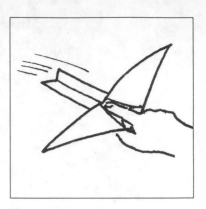

2 Once you have mastered this fold, hold a class discussion about airplane design and aerodynamics (the study of air forces). Try to gather some material on this interesting subject, which combines both science and art.

3 Next, pass out the materials, and fold the flicker together.

4 After the children have learned the fold, encourage them to experiment by cutting movable wing flaps, like the figure to the right. They should also decorate their planes using pencils and markers. Since this is but one of many ways to make paper planes, ask them to try a few others.

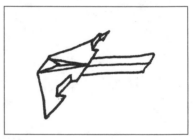

5 Finally, when all the planes are complete, hold a flying contest in a large room or on the playing field to see whose plane travels the greatest distance. To promote eye safety, have all the students line up, away from the flight direction, so that no one gets injured by a plane.

Notes: *Although paper airplanes are often frowned at, they can be a wonderful source of scientific and artistic discovery and delight. Over the years, I have found that children quickly understand and pick up on such ideas. They become serious designers and experimenters, when you, the teacher, treat such a topic seriously.*

When my wife does this activity, she also incorporates a discussion on important figures of flight, such as Leonardo da Vinci, the Wright Brothers, and Sally Ride. The crucial message is that people must "fool around" with materials and ideas to make new contributions. This is a thought that we should all fly with!

Imaginary Vegetables

A Garden Full of Surprises

Purpose: *To design and create imaginary vegetables with distinct characters*

Materials:
Colored construction paper (12" x 18"), assorted paper scraps, white glue, scissors, pencils, markers.

Description: *Just imagine for a moment being transported to a mysterious garden filled with many unique and unusual vegetables. What would you find in such a place? How would these growing things look? Would they talk or sing? Would they have faces, arms, and legs? These are a few of the questions that could launch this activity.*

1 You might begin the activity by presenting your class with a situation and questions like those listed above. You may also wish to show the children some sample imaginary vegetables that you made.

2 After the kids have caught the spirit of the lesson, invite them to create their own imaginary vegetables. They may wish to sketch their ideas on scrap paper before using cut paper or they may want to experiment using different pieces of cut paper.

3 Pass out the materials and let them begin working. You should walk about the room during this time to give individual advice and encouragement. Be sure to remind the students that they should make more than one vegetable.

4 When all the students are finished, create an imaginary vegetable garden representing the entire class. Don't forget to design vines and leaves to accompany your vegetables. Such a garden can sprout from a classroom or hall bulletin board and can grow larger with additional vegetable sessions.

Notes: *As I recall my father's vegetable garden, I realize that a good gardener is something of a magician. Indeed, wandering in a thriving garden is a wonderful experience, and wandering in an imaginary one should be even more interesting.*

After the children have finished their garden, you might wish to correlate it with a language arts experience. Ask the students in your class to write original stories about their vegetables and the entire garden. You will see ideas growing and imaginations flowering on all sides.

123

Letter or Number Designs

The Magic of Symbols

Purpose: *To use letters and numbers as a basis for creating visual designs*

Materials:
Newsprint and white drawing paper (9" x 12"), rulers, compasses, pencils, colored pencils, markers.

Description: *The different shapes of various letters and numbers are fascinating to contemplate. The idea of using visual symbols with special connections to language and math systems is one of the miracles of humanity. In this activity, we will be using both letters and numbers.*

1 Begin the activity by holding a discussion on the amazing shapes of letters and numbers. You may wish to bring several lettering books to class to illustrate some of the vast variety of lettering styles. In addition, you might show and discuss some already completed letter or number designs.

2 Next, explain that in this activity each person will choose a letter or number as a basis for his/her design. This letter or number can be drawn in any style that pleases the individual student, and, for letters, can be either lower or upper case. However, it is important that each letter or number be drawn in open-block fashion (𝔸) rather than with a single line (A).

In addition, the letter or number should show variety in terms of size (small, medium, and large) and direction. The completed design should, in fact, be infinite, with letters or numbers stretching off the 9″ x 12″ sheet. The letters or numbers should be transparent and should overlap and intersect with one another for interest.

3 You may wish to use the chalkboard to demonstrate some of these points:

4 After the design drawing is complete, select a color and begin coloring a small section of your design. When you reach the boundaries of the next section, change to a second color. In some situations, a third color may also be necessary.

5 Once the children understand the concept, pass out the materials and let them begin work. They should make some preliminary sketches on the newsprint before using the white drawing paper.

6 When all the designs are complete, hold a sharing session and exhibition.

Notes: *This activity is rather like getting involved in putting together an interesting puzzle. I was first introduced to it many years ago in one of Dale Stein's design classes. Since the design is infinite, and the letters or numbers are transparent, the artist becomes immersed in a strange land that extends in all directions. A fascinating variation to filling in the different shapes with color is to fill them in with distinct patterns, such as stars or flowers.*

Since the activity is thought-provoking and time-consuming, I recommend the design be no larger than 9" x 12". Even completing a design of this size will take the students a considerable length of time. This activity provides an excellent opportunity for your students to develop a better understanding of how to work with different shapes and colors.

126

Line Designs

The Line is Fine

Purpose: *To create unique patterns using lines*

Materials:
Newsprint and white drawing paper (9" x 12"), rulers, compasses, pencils, colored markers.

Description: *Lines are very exciting things! Although the shortest distance between two points is a straight line, there are many other kinds of lines. Lines can curve, zig-zag, zoom, and linger. They can meander, curl, and wave. Although they often serve as boundaries to shapes and forms, they can also be used to enhance and decorate. By carefully considering the different directions and characteristics that lines can take, and by using lines with varying thicknesses, you can attain intriguing patterns. In this activity, we will focus on the fascinating world of line.*

1 A short class discussion is a fine way to begin the activity. You might ask the children to look around the room and point out noticeable lines. Are these really lines or something else? Discuss.

2 You may also show your students some completed line designs, and talk about some characteristics of line, such as direction, thickness, and decorative potential.

3 After the discussion, pass out the newsprint and ask each child to make some sketches using lines. Use pencils, rulers, and compasses for this purpose. The sketches may be representational or abstract, playful or serious.

4 Next, ask each student to select his/her favorite design and re-draw it on the white drawing paper. Each individual shape within the designs should be decorated with different kinds of lines. For example:

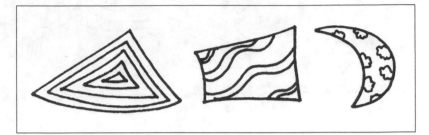

Students should first draw the lines with pencil and then go over them with colored markers. They can, of course, use rulers and compasses.

5 When all of the designs are complete, hold a sharing session and exhibit.

Notes: *This puzzle-like activity is both fun and thought-provoking. It challenges the children to ponder some of the special qualities that lines possess. Remember that anything that is linear can satisfy the goal of this activity. I'm sure your class will surprise you with a wide range of designs, which prove that lines are fine!*

Magazine Drawings

Growing Drawings from Magazine Cuttings

Purpose: *To develop pencil drawings that are connected to magazine photographs or illustrations*

Materials:
Assorted
magazines,
white drawing paper
(9" x 12"),
pencils,
scissors,
white glue.

Description: *Magazines provide hours of information and amusement, but they also contain many fascinating photographs, illustrations, and advertisements that are visually appealing. In this activity, we will be using the art from magazines as a basis for the creation of unusual pencil drawings.*

1 Prior to starting any artwork, ask your students to bring in a selection of magazines. News, nature, and travel magazines are especially useful. You may also wish to bring in some magazines in order to supplement the supply.

2 Next, show and discuss with the students some sample magazine drawings that you have done. They need not be large, but they should be varied. To create such an artwork, use the following procedure:

a. First, select a magazine photograph or illustration that appeals to you, and remove it from the magazine.
b. Cut the photo or illustration in half, in any manner you wish (straight, curved, zig-zag) and glue it onto the 9" x 12" white drawing paper.
c. Finally, using pencil, draw the portion you have removed. The drawing can be in any style you wish and can be similar to or different from the original cutting.

Once you have explained the procedure to your class, distribute the materials and let the students begin working. Be available for individual guidance and consultation during this time.

 When all of the magazine drawings are complete, hold a sharing session and exhibit.

Notes: *The contrast between a glossy magazine cutting and a matte pencil drawing is an especially interesting characteristic of this activity. Keep in mind that the style of the drawings should be as unique as each student. In this regard, some children will make very realistic continuations of their photo or illustration, while others will do abstract or surrealistic things.*

Such an activity is not only valuable in helping to refine drawing skills, but it also sharpens the eye in studying visual detail. The children should enjoy selecting the photograph or illustration, as well as doing the cutting and drawing.

Milk Carton Monsters

A Half-Gallon of Fun

Purpose: *To create a fantasy creature based on an empty container*

Materials:
Rinsed milk cartons (half-gallon size preferred), colored construction paper, found objects (yarn scraps, feathers, pipe cleaners, buttons), pencils, scissors, rulers, markers, white glue.

Description: *"Milk Carton Monsters" should stimulate a feeling of playfulness and experimentation on the part of your students. Indeed, the idea of using an empty container as the foundation for an unusual creature should spark considerable interest. In addition to using many varied materials, it is important to remember that the empty cartons need not be used only in an upright position.*

1 A large supply of empty and thoroughly washed milk or juice cartons is necessary for this activity. Therefore, remind the children to bring these containers from home.

2 Once you have gathered the necessary materials, you should hold a class discussion on creating fantasy creatures. What would such a creature look like? Would it be friendly or mean? Would it have teeth or no mouth at all? Questions such as these might provide some interesting food for thought.

3 You may also wish to show your class several completed milk-carton monsters that you have created. Hold a discussion of how the various materials were used.

4 Next, briefly describe how to cover the empty carton with construction paper. It is more effective to use paper rather than tempera paint for covering the carton, since the paint does not adhere well to the waxed cardboard. In order to simplify the process, use pre-cut pieces of paper in various colors. It is easier to cover each panel of the carton separately.

5 Decorations and characterizations of each milk carton should be left to the whim of each child. Point out to the children that they should experiment with the placement of materials before gluing anything in place on their cartons.

6 Next, distribute the various materials and let the creations begin! Be available to assist the children with any problems that might arise.

7 After each child has completed his/her creation, initiate a monster introduction session followed by an exhibit.

Notes: *"Milk Carton Monsters" are intriguing because they enable the children to utilize found objects in their creative endeavors. They also motivate kids to rely on their own imaginations as the source for new creatures.*

Since these monsters are very sturdy and have excellent bases, they make wonderful shelf guardians or library protectors. Such guardians can stand alone or be grouped on high shelves and window ledges. Try to supply a wide range of found objects and scrap materials in order to diversify the appearance of each monster.

The monsters that result from this activity will have a variety of different looks and personalities. This fact lends itself to correlation with writing and language arts. In this connection, you might ask each student to write a story about his/her monster and display the stories with the artwork.

Money Designs

A Penny for Your Thoughts

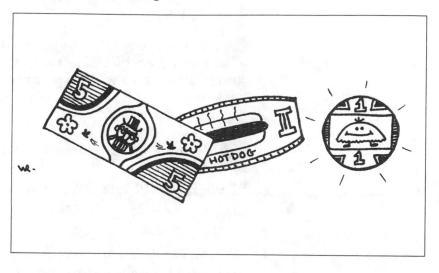

Purpose: *To design new currency for a real or imaginary country*

Materials:
Newsprint and white drawing paper (9" x 12"), pencils, colored markers, watercolors, brushes, plastic cups, water, newspaper, white glue.

Description: *Although money is a necessity, it is also a fascinating study in art and design. We seem to become most aware of this fact when we come in contact with currency from other lands. Somehow we tend to look at it more closely and study it with different eyes. Our own currency, however, also has some wonderful designs and contains some very curious details, of which only coin collectors are usually aware.*

In this activity, you will be asking your students to design an original bill or coin for any country or for a land that exists only in their imaginations.

1 You can begin the activity by showing and discussing a selection of currency from our country and other places in the world. You might also include some money that you have designed. During your discussion be sure to point out that artists are strongly involved in designing money.

2 Next, ask each student to formulate a design for his/her own coin or bill. Explain that these designs can represent money from here, there, or anywhere. They can also be made in a variety of sizes and shapes and use many color combinations.

3 At this point, distribute the 9" x 12" newsprint and ask the students to make some sketches of their coins or bills.

4 After each child has decided on a favorite design, pass out the rest of the materials and have the students transfer and color their work on the white drawing paper.

5 When the final designs are dry, they can be cut from the white paper into the shape desired. The students may also wish to do another design on the back or draw and paint a second design and glue it to the back of the first.

6 When all of the money is complete, a show is definitely in order. Perhaps a local bank might be interested in such an exhibit.

Notes: *The design of money is very fascinating, and if you are located near a government mint, you might consider making a class visit. My wife and I have often brought school groups to the Franklin Mint in Philadelphia. Not only are the children interested in seeing the coins glittering along the conveyer belts, but they also gain knowledge about the design of coins and medals.*

I believe that you will find, as I have, that the children will create all sorts of wonderful money. You will see coins and bills of all sizes and descriptions, with strange animals, kids' faces, and unusual presidents and kings. Indeed, although this new money may be counterfeit, the learning experience is worth its weight in gold.

Monoprints

One-of-a-Kind Prints

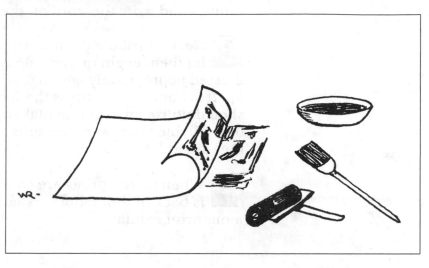

Purpose: *To create a print by painting on a flat, hard surface*

Materials:
Manila and white drawing paper (12" x 18" or 18" x 24"), tempera paints (assorted colors), plastic cups, aluminum trays, brushes, sponges, brayers, paint rollers, a bucket of water, hard surface (formica desk or table top, plexiglass or acetate sheet).

Description: *There is something very stimulating about painting directly on a desk, table top, or piece of plexiglass, and then carefully pulling a print from such a painting. This activity centers around these pursuits and requires an open, flexible approach. Since much is left to chance in monoprints, the students learn how to compromise between working directly and working with the effects of indirect unknown forces.*

1 Begin this activity by having your class gather around you for a brief demonstration of the monoprint process:

a. Use a large formica-topped table, desk, or a piece of plexiglass, and quickly apply some tempera paint in any style or pattern you wish. You can use brushes, sponges, brayers, paint rollers, or a combination of these implements for this purpose.

b. Next, while the painting is still wet, place a sheet of manila or white drawing paper over the painting and gently rub the back of the paper.

c. Carefully pull the paper away from the painted surface, and take a look at the print that appears on your paper. This is the basic idea of monoprints. The table or desk top can be cleaned easily with a sponge and water.

2 After your demonstration, ask the children to return to their seats and hold a question-and-answer period. Introduce the concept of "monoprints," and write the word on the chalkboard.

3 Next, distribute the materials to the students, and let them begin to work. Be certain they are dressed appropriately and that all sleeves are rolled up. It is important to stress the fact that the paintings should utilize an experimental approach. You should be available to answer questions and solve problems as they arise.

4 When all the prints are complete, and the room is back in order, hold a sharing session and monoprint exhibit.

Notes: *Monoprints can be messy, and they require a flexible approach on the part of both the students and teacher. To expedite the process, let the students take turns working on their prints at four large tables, rather than everyone using her/his own desk. Although each student will produce only one print per painting, she/he may wish to re-work the same desktop painting several times, thus creating a related series of monoprints.*

I have found that using large paper (18" x 24" or larger) can be especially intriguing for the children. In this case, of course, you will need a large desk or tabletop for your painting. In addition, the children should be encouraged to try a variety of different painting applicators and should experiment with different hand pressures while painting.

It is important in this activity to motivate your students to be both flexible and inventive. You, as the teacher, should also work in this same spirit. When the prints are dry, the students might also wish to draw on them using colored markers. Monoprints are joyful and challenging and are a definite crowd pleaser!

New Alphabets

Creating ABCs

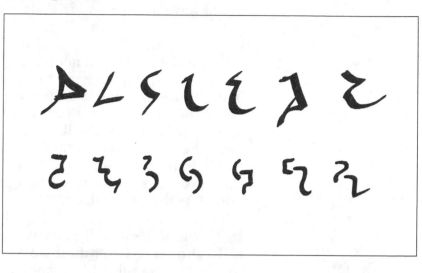

Purpose: *To better understand the influence of artistic design on alphabet characters*

Materials:
*Manila paper
(9" x 12"),
white drawing
paper,
(4" x 12"),
pencils,
rulers,
colored markers,
India ink,
brushes,
newspaper.*

Description: *Different alphabets are very exciting to look at, whether one understands them or not. When one looks closely at the various characters or letters, it becomes apparent that each of them relies on specific designs. In fact, one of the hallmarks of humanity is that we have devised special groups of symbols to communicate ideas across our world and over time.*

In this activity, we will be focusing on the development of new alphabets, or a new system of characters to represent writing and speech. What will such an alphabet look like? How will each character be written and pronounced? These questions should be kept in mind as the children proceed to work.

1 This activity might be best launched by referring your students to the Table of Alphabets in a standard dictionary. Hold a discussion on some of these alphabets, and ask the children how they are different from our own. For example: How does the letter "A" differ in Hebrew, Greek, and Arabic?

2 After your discussion, ask your students to pretend they are in an imaginary country that has no alphabet. It is the responsibility of each child to design and develop an alphabet for this country. Remind the children that the designs shouldn't be too complicated and that each letter should look different.

Distribute the manila paper and pencils and let the students begin to sketch some ideas. They can use their dictionaries and any lettering books you might have available to stimulate their thinking.

 Once the children have devised their complete alphabets on the manila paper, they are ready to transfer their alphabets to the white drawing paper. The children should use their rulers to form guidelines on the white paper before doing any lettering. These lines will better enable the students to keep the alphabetic characters at a uniform size. All preliminary designs should be done in pencil. Students may also use several sheets of 4″ x 12″ paper to complete their alphabets.

 When the pencil designs are done, the students should re-letter their work using colored markers or black India ink and brushes.

 Conclude the activity with a final sharing session and alphabet exhibit.

Notes: *Letters can be very beautiful and very diverse: They may reflect the qualities of flowing Arabic characters in a mosque, the fantastic print of a medieval manuscript, the marvelous characters of a Hebrew tract, the wonderful symbols of our Declaration of Independence, or the graceful writing of a Japanese scroll. Each letter is a visual design with a special sound and meaning.*

At one time we concentrated on penmanship, with the idea that each student should perfect his/her facility at forming alphabetic characters. Indeed, this practice still continues in some places. In any event, this activity gives the students a chance to realize the relationship between good design and the formation of letters. Perhaps, even more significantly, it gives the children a chance to contemplate the amazing idea of using special symbols to communicate.

At the conclusion of this activity, ask each child to think up a special name for his/her new language. Such names can be based on either the first or last name of the inventor. For example: Jillian, Henryish, Brownic, or Smithish!

Nothing Machines

Crazy Contraptions

Purpose: *To design and create a novel machine that does nothing*

Materials:
*Manila paper
(9" x 12"),
empty cartons and
containers,
used spools of
thread,
bottle and tube
caps,
buttons,
pipe cleaners,
colored
construction paper,
paper fasteners,
paper clips,
yarn,
string,
white glue,
scissors,
pencils,
markers.*

Description: *Although machines are generally built to fulfill a function and help make our lives more livable, this is often not the case. In this activity, we pay homage to the idea that some machines are good for nothing by attempting to build a nothing machine. The crucial thing to remember is that each child's imagination must reign supreme, and that all creations should be both useless and fun!*

1 In order to do this activity effectively, a lot of empty containers, bottle caps, buttons, and found objects are necessary. Hold a collection campaign before actually beginning the activity. Once you and your class have accumulated an assortment of goodies, you are ready to go.

2 Next, bring in several nothing machines and show them to your class. Hold a discussion on the purpose of nothing machines, and get the students thinking about designing their own silly contraptions.

3 Pass out some manila sketching paper, and let the children make some preliminary drawings if they wish. Then distribute the previously collected materials and let the work begin.

4 Encourage each designer to position his/her materials before gluing them in place. This will enable the students to change their designs before making them permanent.

5 When all the materials on all the machines have been glued into position, and all drawing, stringing, and clipping is complete, hold a special exhibit. Each machine may be shown separately, or the class may wish to position all of the works so that the pieces form a single giant nothing machine.

Notes: *Above all else, this activity relies on a sense of imagination and humor. Over the years, I have seen children build some of the most creative, unusual, and fun nothing machines. These machines have had propellers, wheels, gears, antennas, and all sorts of strange parts.*

If you are lucky enough to live near a recycling center or factory complex, you may be able to obtain some very interesting scrap materials for little or no money. In the Recycling Center of the Boston Children's Museum, I recently filled a large shopping bag with some wonderful plastic computer keys, bottle tops, foam scraps, ribbons, and strings for a very small fee. Such items are excellent for a nothing machine activity, adding a great amount of curiosity and interest!

Optical Illusion Designs

Now "Eye" See It—Now "Eye" Don't

Purpose: *To create designs that dazzle the eye*

Materials:
Newsprint and white drawing paper (9" x 12"), pencils, markers, compasses, protractors, rulers.

Description: *Illusions play strange tricks on the eye. Anyone who has ever been in the desert or driven down a long road in the heat of summer has probably seen a "mirage." This mysterious illusion of shimmering water vanishes, of course, as one draws closer to it.*

Artists often use illusion in their works. Probably the most outstanding example of this occurs with the use of perspective, where the illusion of three-dimensional space is created on a flat surface. In more recent times, the "Op Art" movement was composed of a variety of painted illusions based on geometry and optics. In this activity, we will be concentrating on creating optical illusions that fool the eyes and puzzle the mind.

1 Prior to starting this activity with your class, collect some reference books and prints dealing with optical illusions. You can locate materials at the library by looking up "Op Art." You might also look up specific artists, such as Escher, Vasarely, and Agam. In addition, create a few illusions of your own to gain a clearer understanding of the topic.

2 Next, present the theme of "Optical Illusions" to your class, and incorporate the books, prints, and illusions you have gathered and created. Hold a discussion about such illusions, and explain that such artwork can be geometric, free-form, or a combination of the two. Point out that when you employ combinations of simple designs, such as spirals, crosses, squares, rectangles, triangles, and floral and leaf shapes, amazing things can happen.

3 Distribute the newsprint to the students and let them sketch some different design ideas in pencil.

4 Then ask each person to choose his/her favorite illusion and re-draw it on the white drawing paper. He or she should color the lines and shapes (alternating) with markers. The work need not be large. In fact, due to the puzzle-like aspect, a smaller size (9″ x 12″ or less) is best.

5 Conclude the activity by holding a sharing session and exhibition.

142

Notes: *Optical illusions can become quite time-consuming and involved. Therefore, be sure to advise your students to keep their designs simple. Once the children get involved in this activity, you can be certain they will have lots of fun. Not only are intersecting lines interesting, but they become even more exciting with the introduction of alternating areas of color.*

As the illusions progress, they have an almost hypnotic effect for both the artist and viewer. In this connection, it is a fine activity to relate to a study of science, psychology, and optics. Indeed, such designs will intrigue the mind as they dazzle the eye!

Paper Scoring

Purpose: *To create three-dimensional forms from flat sheets of paper using the scoring technique*

143

Materials:

White drawing and colored construction paper (9"x12"), pencils, scissors, rulers, white glue, spools of thread, needles.

Description: *Folding can turn flat sheets of paper into interesting forms, and scoring enables even more exciting things to happen. The term "scoring" simply refers to a line that has been scratched into the surface of the paper. Although scoring lines can be straight, they can also be curved in interesting ways. Once you have scored a line into the paper, you can obtain fantastic shapes by simply folding along it.*

In this activity, we will be experimenting and creating using this special technique. In addition, the shapes and forms that result can be assembled into either a paper sculpture or a mobile.

1 A fine way to begin this activity is to conduct a short demonstration of paper scoring. Ask the children if they know the meaning of scoring. Then, using some flat pieces of paper, show your class how scoring works.

a. First, take a sheet of paper and draw a line across it using your pencil and ruler.

b. Next, open your scissors and grasp one of the scissor points like a pencil or pen. Then, using this point, gently scratch along the line in a continuous motion. You may wish to use your ruler as a guide.

c. Now gently fold along the line you have scored. You should achieve a very crisp, neat fold.

d. Try the same technique with a curved line, and see what happens. As you know, under normal circumstances a curved line is impossible to fold, but with scoring it works amazingly well.

e. The forms you have created can now be glued together to make a sculptural object or strung together to make a mobile. If you wish to create a sculpture, be sure to experiment with the positioning of the forms before gluing. To create a mobile, thread your needle and stitch the forms together, making certain all knots and stitches are tight.

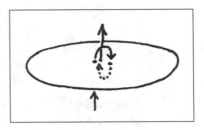

2 Distribute the materials to your class after your demonstration and let the work begin. Be available for questions and/or problems as they arise.

3 Hold a sharing session and exhibit when all of the works are complete.

Notes: *I find the most amazing aspect of this activity is being able to score and fold ordinary sheets of paper into wonderful curving forms. The children you work with will probably also be intrigued by this special quality of paper scoring. Be sure to encourage each individual to experiment with different scored lines in an effort to create new and exciting shapes.*

Once the students understand the fundamentals of paper scoring, they can apply it to many other art activities. In fact, scored paper shapes can be incorporated into mask designs and puppet making. The wonderful effects that begin with a simple scratch on a piece of paper will get a high "score" from any artist!

Record Covers

Adding a Musical Note

Purpose: *To create an attractive cover design for a musical selection of your choice*

Materials:
*Manila paper
(9" x 12"),
white drawing paper
(pre-cut sizes for
cassette recording
boxes, compact disc
packages, and
albums),
rulers,
compasses,
pencils,
markers,
watercolors,
brushes,
plastic cups,
water,
newspaper.*

Description: *Musical recordings are a wonderful experience for people of all ages, and children are no exception. By becoming aware of your students' musical interests, you can gain a better understanding of them. In this activity, we will be concentrating on cover designs for records, cassette tapes, and compact discs.*

1 Begin this activity with a general discussion about music and musical groups. Ask the children what kinds of music they enjoy the most. Who sings or performs this music? How many students like rock, rap, classical, jazz, folk, opera, or show tunes?

2 After you have discussed these things, show and talk about some examples of cover designs for musical recordings. Then, ask each student to consider a recording that he/she likes and design an attractive cover for it. If a student has no ideas, you might ask him/her to make up an imaginary musical artist, group, or composition. If you were a musician, what kind of music would you make? What would your newest release look like?

3 Pass out the manila paper, and ask the children to sketch some of their ideas in pencil.

4 Next, have them choose one idea and transfer it to the pre-cut white drawing paper. Rulers, compasses, markers, and watercolors can also be used at this time. All lettering should utilize simple pencil guidelines to insure better presentation.

5 When all the designs are complete, hold a discussion and exhibition.

Notes: *This activity stimulates the children to consider an important area in their lives. Each of us has favorite musical selections and sounds that add dimension and meaning to our world. By creating visual designs for these special things, we are focusing on an important aspect of our uniqueness as individuals.*

Designs can be done in any style or colors that the individual may choose. The completed covers will make a thoughtful hall display that will attract both interest and comment. You may also wish to correlate this activity with written compositions on why each child likes the musical selection or group he/she chose. These compositions can be displayed along with the visual designs.

Scrap Wood Sculptures

From Scrap Pile to Gallery

Purpose: *Creating additive sculptures from assorted pieces of scrap wood*

Materials:
A large supply of wood scraps, sandpaper, files, hammers, nails (assorted sizes), white glue, tempera paints, plastic cups, brushes, newspaper, safety goggles.

Description: *When we look carefully at the items we toss away in our society, we often find many fascinating things. Pieces of scrap wood are a fine example of this phenomenon. Indeed, assorted odds and ends cut from lumber or branches have a great deal of sculptural potential.*

In this activity, we will be using a variety of scrap wood pieces to create unique and unusual sculptures.

1 The first step in preparing for this activity is to gather an abundant supply of scrap wood. Armed with a few empty cardboard boxes from the supermarket, make a visit to your local lumber yard. Explain to the owner or manager that you plan to do a sculpture project with your class, and ask if he/she would be willing to donate some wood scraps from the milling area. Most merchants are happy to aid in a local school project. You or your friends may also have a good supply of scrap wood at home.

2 After gathering the wood, build a few scrap wood sculptures at home to get the feel of this activity. Select a variety of interesting pieces and experiment with different configurations before gluing or nailing the wood in place. You are now ready to begin the activity with your class.

3 Launch the class presentation by showing and discussing the scrap wood sculptures that you made. Explain that these sculptures are "additive" rather than "subtractive." Ask the children what these terms mean. (In "additive" sculptures, we are constructing the sculpture by adding different parts, while in "subtractive" sculpture, we are making a sculpture by taking pieces away.) Point out to the kids that each sculpture they make should be unique.

4 At this time it is a good idea to discuss the safety procedures that apply to using a hammer and nails. Hold a short demonstration stressing the use of safety goggles and care of hands and fingers.

5 Next, distribute the materials to the students and let them commence working. It is important to let each student choose from a wide variety of wood pieces—therefore, having lots of wood is imperative. As the children work, be available for individual guidance.

6 When all the hammering and gluing is complete, students can paint and decorate the sculptures.

7 At the end of the activity, hold a discussion and display.

Notes: *Scrap wood sculptures are both challenging and fun. You should be aware that they will take several sessions to complete, so be prepared. After the works are on display, you may wish to invite the local lumber merchant to the exhibit. As an alternate plan, send her/him some photos of the works and thank-you letters from both you and your students. Through such small gestures of courtesy, you can help cultivate an important long-term tradition.*

Single-Sheet Constructions

The Potential of Plain Paper

Purpose: *To create an experimental design with a single piece of paper through cutting, folding, and bending*

Materials:

White, black, and colored construction paper (12" x 18"), scissors, white glue.

Description: *A single sheet of paper has enormous potential. It can be used for a wide variety of creative endeavors, including painting, drawing, writing, and flying. In this activity, we will be cutting, folding, bending, and curling pieces of paper into sculptural constructions. The activity requires very few materials and lots of imagination.*

1 Before starting the activity with your class, experiment with the idea yourself.

Take a single sheet of 12" x 18" white, black, or colored construction paper. Then, using your scissors, cut some straight and/or curved lines into your paper from different sides and directions.

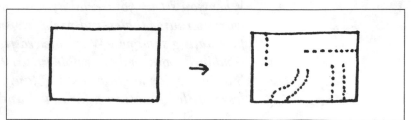

Next, fold, roll, bend, or curl these strips into new and different shapes and glue them to the same sheet.

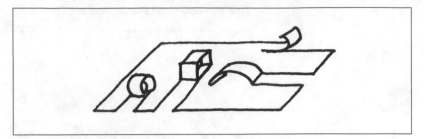

When you have made and fastened as many shapes as you wish, glue the single-sheet construction to a background sheet of a contrasting color.

2 Next, hold a class discussion on the potentials of paper with your children. Ask them for feedback on what things paper can be used for. Then show the class some sample works you have created and discuss how you developed such works. As you do this presentation, try showing your constructions under a single light or spotlight—the effects of the shadows can be especially interesting.

3 After the discussion, distribute the supplies to your class, and let them begin work.

4 A concluding sharing session and exhibit should complete the activity.

Notes: *Single-sheet constructions are especially valuable for teaching children that three-dimensional forms can be created from two-dimensional surfaces. They are also great for programs with very few art supplies. It is important to encourage your students to be imaginative and risky in cutting, folding, and curling their papers.*

When you set up your exhibit, you may want to place the works on large tables and use a few small lights to create fascinating shadows. When viewed from different angles, the combined works may resemble futuristic cities or landscapes. Such a display might be used to launch a creative writing lesson titled, "Lost in a Strange Land."

150

Space Painting

Purpose: *To design and paint a new place in space*

Materials:
*Newsprint (9" x 12"),
white drawing paper
(12" x 18"),
pencils,
markers,
watercolors,
brushes,
newspaper,
plastic cups,
water.*

Description: *Human beings have always been curious about what is beyond the boundaries of our planet. Are there other worlds and other beings? What would they look like? Although space exploration by our country is progressing, we can only imagine answers to these questions. In this activity, we will be tapping our powers of imagination to draw and paint scenes from space.*

151

1 Before introducing the idea to your class, try to gather a variety of books, posters, and magazines that focus on space. Your local library, science museum, or planetarium are all fine places to look.

2 After gathering your materials, hold a discussion on space with your students. You might ask them some of the questions listed above. Show a variety of visual materials to enhance your discussion.

3 Next ask the class to make some sketches on newsprint of what they believe space would be like. Needless to say, rockets, flying saucers, meteorites, and star clusters are but some of the phenomena you might expect.

4 When the children have done several sketches, ask each student to choose her/his favorite and transfer it to the 12" x 18" white drawing paper using pencil. They can then color or paint the drawing using markers and watercolors.

5 Hold a final discussion and exhibition when all the paintings have been completed.

Notes: *Children are always intrigued by the mystery and magic of space. Since the topic is so vast and so little known, it enables everyone to really stretch their imaginations. Because the entertainment industry has done a great deal with space, playing the soundtracks from films on space might provide interesting music by which to work.*

In addition to creating some thoughtful artwork, this activity can also be easily coupled with language arts. Ask your students to write a story about their work or to compose poems about space. The study of our own astronauts and space explorers can also provide vital links to science and social studies. Indeed, this topic provides lots of space for expansion!

Sponge Painting

Soaking up the Fun

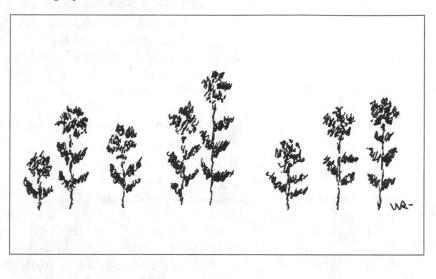

Purpose: *To utilize sponges and sponge pieces in creating tempera paintings*

Materials:

Sponges and sponge pieces, manila and white drawing paper (12" x 18"), tempera paints (assorted colors), aluminum trays or pie tins, newspaper, scissors.

Description: *The particular implement that one uses to apply paint to a surface has a distinct effect on the overall look and feeling of the artwork. This is especially true when one uses a sponge rather than a brush. In this activity, we will focus on using such a non-traditional item in the painting process. Although sponges are generally used to absorb spills, we will be employing them to apply colors in many unique ways.*

1 In order to conduct this activity effectively, you need a generous supply of sponges. Therefore, obtaining several large packages of sponges from a local supermarket is important before beginning to work. These sponges should be of varied sizes, so it is a good idea to cut them accordingly using scissors.

2 Next, you should experiment with some sponge painting of your own to soak up some insights about this activity.

a. First, prepare your working area for painting. If you are resting your paper on a formica surface, there is little need to cover it with newspaper.

b. Next, pour a little tempera paint into a shallow aluminum tray or pie plate. You should have several of these trays to accommodate various colors of tempera.

c. Then, using your sponges, begin applying the paint to the manila or white drawing paper. In the first painting, try to use the sponge in as many different ways as you can. Try stippling, dotting, brushing, and rolling. Also, try using one color over another, and notice what happens.

d. Do several paintings in any style or on any subject you wish. You are now ready to begin working with your class.

 Present your students with the activity by holding a discussion on painting, and point out how different paint applicators can create different effects.

 After being sure that all sleeves are rolled up and all tables or desks are ready, pass out the materials and let the children begin to work. Be sure to stress the experimental aspect of working with sponges. Encourage each student to try using the sponges in different ways and to create individualistic works.

 When the room is cleaned up and the paintings are dry, hold a sharing session and exhibit.

Notes: *The idea of using varied items to create works of art is not a new idea. The fact is that artists are often pathfinders in material experimentation. In many instances, such experiments simply involve using implements from a different task in the art process. The use of sponges is a fine example.*

In an effort to build on such a notion, you might encourage your students to try painting with other objects that are generally used for something else. Sponge painting provides an excellent opportunity for students to accumulate some exciting knowledge while they soak up the fun!

Storybooks

Insights Through Words and Pictures

Purpose: *To design and create an original illustrated storybook*

Materials:
*Manila paper
(9" x 12"),
white drawing and
colored
construction paper
(individually cut),
assorted cardboard
or poster board,
pencils,
rulers,
compasses,
hole punch,
scissors,
yarn,
paper fasteners,
crayons,
colored markers,
watercolors,
brushes,
white glue,
plastic cups,
water,
newspaper.*

Description: *Anyone who has ever read stories to children or browsed in the children's section of a library or bookshop knows about the fascinating world of illustrated storybooks. Such books are as delightful as they are diverse. Indeed, the wonderful illustrations that embellish children's literature often make books for adults pale by comparison.*

In this activity, we will be focusing on writing and illustrating original picture storybooks. Each child will be both an author and artist who will be creating a book for younger readers.

1 Your first step should be to make a visit to your school or local library to select a variety of children's storybooks. Make sure that the storylines are not too involved and that the illustrations are simple and attractive. It's also important to gather a number of books in a variety of artistic styles (realistic, abstract, etc.).

2 Next, bring these books to class, and explain to your students that you would like each of them to write and illustrate a picture storybook for a younger sibling, relative, or friend. Be sure to point out that these stories should be clear and simple.

3 Then read the selected storybooks to your students and hold a discussion on children's stories. After your discussion, ask each child to think about and jot down some ideas for his/her own storybook. Encourage original stories rather than simply retelling known stories. The stories can be based on a countless number of things, including lost shoes, new bikes, old houses, and small dogs.

4 When the students have all chosen their favorite stories, distribute the 9″ x 12″ manila paper, and ask each child to make a grid-like pattern with a pencil and ruler. This will effectively divide the 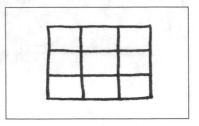 paper into a number of smaller rectangles, as shown to the right. Each of these small rectangles will represent one page of a book. If more space is needed, advise your students to create a second grid on another piece of manila paper.

5 Next, print the story in the appropriate boxes and draw rough illustrations to correlate with each part of the story. Make your students aware that where they place their illustrated designs and print-lines will make a difference in how the finished story will look. Suggest the use of variety in page designs.

6 When the grid sketches are completed, the students can begin transferring their designs to the white drawing or colored construction paper. Each student should decide what size they would like their books to be and measure and cut the pages accordingly. In addition, each individual must decide what materials she/he will be using to do their illustrations—crayons, cut paper, markers, watercolors, etc.

7 After the children have created their illustrations on the good copy, have them draw some light pencil guidelines for the written story. They should lightly print the words in pencil before going over them in marker.

8 When all the pages are complete, each student should measure and cut a back and front cover using the cardboard or poster board. The front cover should also be attractively designed and lettered.

9 Using the hole punch, perforate the cover and pages and attach them with paper fasteners or yarn.

10 A story hour is the natural and exciting conclusion for this activity. This allows each student an opportunity to share her/his story with the entire class. A book display in the school or local public library is also an excellent follow-up activity.

Notes: *Although picture storybooks take a considerable amount of time, they are well worth the effort. I was first introduced to this idea many years ago in a course with art educator Susan Wisherd. Since that time, thousands of my students have been designing and creating illustrated storybooks.*

The most exciting part of the activity is the amazing diversity that the children demonstrate. I have had kids write books about all kinds of things, from the very humorous to the very serious. One of my favorite stories was written many years ago by a fifth-grade girl. The story concerned a rude shoe in a repair shop, which kept sticking its tongue out whenever the shoemaker would go to work on it. The shoemaker finally gave up and returned the shoe to its owner, claiming it was too discourteous to work on.

This activity will not only be a hit with your students, but it will also provide you with some excellent insights into them. In addition, you could have your class read their stories to some lower grades in the school. Storybooks have many valuable lessons to impart, so sharpen up your pencil and start writing!

Straw Paintings

They'll Take Your Breath Away

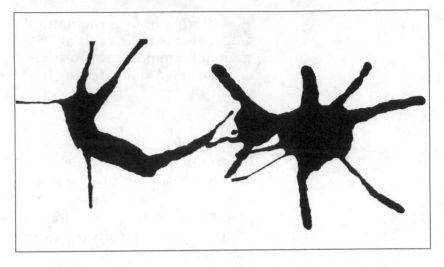

Purpose: *To create tempera paintings through the use of air power*

158

Materials:
Manila paper (12" x 18"), tempera paints (assorted colors), large box of plastic drinking straws, newspaper.

Description: *We've all made paintings using brushes, and we've noticed the particular effect a brush gives as it spreads the paint over a surface. Indeed, different kinds of equipment and everyday objects such as toothbrushes and combs can create a wide variety of results when they are used to apply paint. In this activity, we will be using items that are generally used at the local ice cream shop, the school cafeteria, or on picnics. These items are simple drinking straws.*

1 Straw paintings are fun, but they are also messy. Before starting the activity, be sure the children are dressed accordingly and the table or desk tops are covered with newspaper.

2 Next, hold a brief discussion about straw painting. Mention how different items can create different effects with paint. Explain that in this activity, air will be the vehicle for moving the paint around the paper. Caution the students not to blow too hard or too long through the straws, since it may cause light-headedness. Also mention that they should hold the end of the straw slightly away from the paint and not in it.

3 Distribute the manila paper, straws, and paint. You should be the sole paint supplier. Place several generous drops of paint on each student's paper and ask them to blow the paint around their paper in different directions using the straws. Be sure the paint is thin enough to move easily under breath.

4 While the children work, encourage them to experiment with different amounts of air, and by aiming their straws in various directions. You should also be available to dispense more paint if needed.

5 When all the paintings are completed and dry, hold an exhibition.

Notes: *Painting with straws can literally take your breath away. Therefore, be sure to caution the students to take some "breath breaks" during the working process. Needless to say, the results of straw painting are generally quite abstract and non-representational. However, the paint shapes and spots created can be quite thought-provoking, so you might have each student write a short composition on what her/his painting seems to suggest.*

There is another option that you may also wish to consider. When the initial paintings are dry, distribute markers and ask each student to outline and add different designs to their paintings. These added designs should be inspired by what the original paint splotches suggest. Both of these options make straw paintings not only a very different experience, but a very thoughtful one as well.

159

Styrofoam Monsters

They're Light and Scary

Purpose: *To create a strange creature composed of Styrofoam pieces*

160

Materials:

Styrofoam packing pieces and chips, toothpicks, paper and fabric scraps, yarn, pipe cleaners, buttons, plastic eyes, white glue, plastic picnic knives, scissors, markers.

Description: *Styrofoam is a wonderful packing material, since it is both strong and light. In our present age, whenever something is shipped, one usually finds the new object safely surrounded by Styrofoam pieces. These pieces come in many curious shapes, including peanuts, disks, and varied blocks. By saving these great finds and storing them in large plastic bags, you will accumulate an abundant supply of art materials quickly and easily. The material can be employed in many ways, but, in this activity, we will be using it to build some simple sculptures.*

1 After you have gathered a good supply of Styrofoam, bring it to class along with the other materials mentioned. Explain to the children that we will be building strange Styrofoam sculptures using these things.

2 Before distributing any materials, hold a brief discussion on how Styrofoam pieces can be attached together using white glue and toothpicks. By applying some glue to a toothpick and inserting the pick into the pieces of Styrofoam, you can create a strong and lasting bond. If large pieces of Styrofoam need to be cut before gluing, sawing them with a plastic picnic knife works very well.

Distribute the Styrofoam and other materials, and let your class get to work. Be certain to encourage them to experiment with the material and to use an imaginative approach. In addition, be available to help solve individual design problems as they arise.

4 Once each student has built the basic structure of his/her monster, it is time to add the decorations. Cut paper, fabric, yarn, pipe cleaners, buttons, and plastic eyes are all wonderful additions. It is a good idea to tell your students to glue on these things, rather than simply decorate the Styrofoam only with colored markers.

5 When all the monsters are ready, hold a sharing session and exhibit.

Notes: *Styrofoam monsters are fun to make and help challenge children to use a material that is normally used for another purpose. Since Styrofoam is free and is easy to store, it provides a great vehicle for a wide range of art activities. In addition to monsters, you may wish to consider doing collages, prints, and mobiles.*

The next time you receive a package, remember to save the Styrofoam rather than throw it out. You'll be pleasantly surprised at the fantastic things that can result!

Three-Color Designs

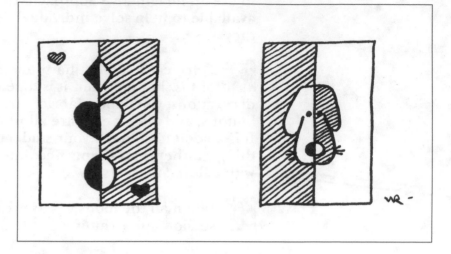

Purpose: *To develop a symmetrical cut-paper design using three colors*

162

Materials:
Assorted colored construction paper (12" x 18"), white glue, scissors.

Description: *In symmetrical arrangements, similar forms or shapes are found on either side of a central dividing line. Symmetry appears all around us, and many natural forms are symmetrical. Artists often use symmetrically balanced compositions or designs in their work. In this activity, we will be focusing on this idea through the creation of cut-paper designs.*

1 Begin the activity by holding a discussion of symmetry and symmetrical objects. Ask your students to name some things around them that are symmetrical. Do we see examples of symmetry in our daily lives? Where? Are people symmetrical?

2 After discussing the concept of symmetry, hold a brief demonstration on how to create a symmetrical design using cut paper.

First, select three colors of 12" x 18" construction paper. Put one sheet aside for the background, and work with the remaining two sheets. Stack the two sheets on top of one another, and line them up evenly.

Then fold the sheets in half in either direction and cut a simple shape from the sheets.

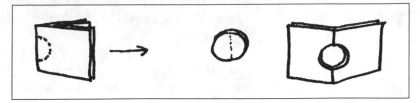

You will now have created four shapes. Two of these shapes are the design you cut, and the other two are the original sheets minus the design. Cut these four shapes in half along the fold line, and place the opposite colored halves on your third sheet of construction paper.

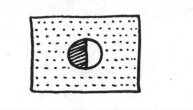

Experiment with the pieces you wish to use before gluing them in place, since, with even a few shapes, there are many possibilities. By cutting a number of shapes from the folded sheets of paper, and by

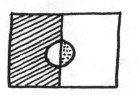

creating additional symmetrical folds, you can make many fascinating designs.

3 When you have completed your simple demonstration, explain to your students that they can cut any shapes they wish, in any style they desire, from their papers.

4 Next, distribute the materials and ask each child to select three different colors and begin work. Be available to assist the students with any problems or questions that may arise.

5 Hold a sharing session and exhibition when all the cut-paper designs are completed.

Notes: *The puzzle-like quality of this activity is thought-provoking and enjoyable. It is a good idea, however, to advise your students to keep their designs simple. This is especially true when the children are doing the activity for the first time.*

The fascinating aspect of three-color designs is that many possibilities present themselves within a very short time using very few shapes. By cutting a number of shapes, the possibilities greatly increase. Once the students understand the principle behind this activity, they will, no doubt, surprise you with some amazing pieces of art.

164

Torn-Paper Designs

Art Through Tearing

Purpose: *To create exciting paper designs from scrap colored construction paper*

Materials:
Assorted colored construction paper (12" x 18") and paper scraps, white glue.

Description: *In many art activities that involve colored construction paper, students generally use scissors. This activity, however, does not include the use of scissors. This fact will probably be the most difficult and challenging aspect for your students. Indeed, I'm quite certain that your students will ask you for scissors again and again. Since one of the major messages of this activity is to introduce children to what can be done by fingers alone, it is very important to keep this experience "scissor free."*

1 Begin this activity with your class by showing and discussing several torn-paper designs. Why are these designs different? What do you notice about them? How were they done?

2 Explain that we will be making torn-paper designs, and that they can be done on any subject or in any style the children wish. The crucial factor is that scissors *cannot* be used. Instead, each student must tear his/her shapes by hand and then glue them into place.

3 Pass out the 12" x 18" colored construction paper and ask each child to select one sheet for her/his background. Then distribute the scrap colored paper and glue.

4 Encourage each child to work carefully and to be as original as possible. Be available to answer any questions as they arise.

5 When the designs are complete, hold a sharing session and exhibit.

Notes: *Probably every classroom in America has a scrap box of old and semi-used colored construction paper pieces. This activity is an ideal way of utilizing this material in an exciting manner.*

Although the children may initially balk at not being able to use scissors, it is amazing how quickly they adjust. In addition, the manual dexterity of many children is downright fascinating. Once the kids get into this activity, they can create wonderful landscapes, animals, and abstract patterns, among other things.

Torn-paper designs give the students a tremendous opportunity to be creative under very restricted conditions and to become aware of recycling materials. They can also contribute to increasing the flexibility and bolstering the self-confidence of children.

Underwater Painting

Looking Beneath the Surface

Purpose: *To create paintings that focus on the underwater world*

Materials:
**Manila paper
(9" x 12"),
white drawing paper
(12" x 18"),
pencils,
markers,
watercolors,
brushes,
water,
water cups,
newspaper.**

Description: *The world under the sea is a marvelous realm of mystery and adventure. It is a place filled with many secrets, which makes it all the more fascinating to contemplate and investigate. In this activity, we will be concentrating on this world under water and making unique paintings about it.*

1 Before introducing this activity to your class, gather some underwater reference books at the library. Magazines such as *National Geographic* and *Natural History,* and your own personal shell collection, if you have one, can also be fine sources of motivation.

2 Bring the reference materials you have gathered to class, and launch a discussion about the amazing world under the water. Ask your students if they have ever done any snorkeling or diving. It is also helpful to make a list on the chalkboard of some of the things that we might find underwater. Explain that the students will be creating individual paintings on this theme.

3 Next, distribute the 9" x 12" manila paper and pencils, and ask the children to do some preliminary sketches of their ideas before doing any painting. Then, have each student select her/his favorite drawing and transfer it to the 12" x 18" white drawing paper.

4 After the drawings have been transferred to the larger paper, pass out the markers, watercolors, and brushes, and let the children begin to paint.

5 When the paintings are complete, hold a sharing session and exhibit.

Notes: *The underwater world seems to hold a special fascination for all of us. The idea of wonderful animals, plants, and geography hidden beneath the surface of the water is exciting to consider. If you have been fortunate enough to do any underwater investigating, be certain to discuss it with your class. Over the years, I have been able to obtain some excellent underwater slides from visits to observatories in the Great Barrier Reef and the Red Sea. Such slides can be excellent motivation for this activity.*

In addition to the excitement of creating individual paintings, this activity can also spark interest in a number of other things. It would be a fine way to begin a science lesson on ocean ecology, which could include water pollution and the problems faced by sea creatures. Setting up your own class fish tank and/or making a visit to a nearby aquarium would also provide fine related experiences. As with many activities, "Underwater Paintings" has a great deal of potential, once you look beneath the surface.

168

Washouts

An Imagination Bath

Purpose: *To do art experiments with paint, ink, and water*

Materials:
White drawing paper (12" x 18"),
tempera paints,
brushes,
India ink (varied colors),
plastic cups,
water,
several large plastic buckets or deep trays,
newspaper,
soap,
paper towels.

Description: *If you like to slosh around in water and get your hands and arms well stained with ink and paint, then you'll enjoy washouts. Although the technique is a very ancient one that is somewhat reminiscent of batik, it is extremely fascinating for people of all ages. Long Island painter and friend Gerald Grace utilizes a related technique in his mysterious mixed media paintings. (However, he carries the idea a great deal further by incorporating many other processes.)*

In this activity, we will be concentrating on simple washouts so that the students can learn to appreciate the wonderful effects of natural forces on art.

1 Before starting this project, be sure that the children and room are well prepared. Everything will run along more smoothly if you remember that the activity is a naturally messy and wet one. Therefore, remind the children to wear old clothes, and have an abundant supply of newspapers and paper towels ready. You may also wish to cover the desk or table tops with newspaper prior to starting, as well as putting newspaper on the floor, in non-traffic areas, as places for the wet paintings to dry.

2 Show your students some finished washouts and ask them some questions about these works. How were these paintings done? What materials were used? How old do the paintings look? Hold a brief discussion based on the students' responses.

3 Next, explain the washout process:

a. First, make a tempera painting, in any style and on any subject you wish, on 12″ x 18″ white drawing paper.
b. Once the painting has dried, gently cover over your painting with India ink. Be careful not to brush the ink on with too much force.
c. Next, fill a large bucket or tray about three-quarters full with water. If you are lucky enough to have a sink in your room, fill it with about six inches of water.
d. When the ink is quite dry, take your painting and completely immerse it in the water. If you are using a bucket, you will have to crumple the painting in order to insert it in the bucket. After the painting is completely covered with water, gently wipe along the surface of the paper using your hand or a sponge. You should pull the painting from the water as you are wiping it off.
e. Take the wet painting to the drying area, and lay it flat on the newspaper.

4 Once the students know the process, they are ready to begin. If you do not have a sink in your room, you will need a good supply of water in buckets or trays. In addition, the water will have to be changed after it was been used a number of times.

5 After the paintings are dry, hold a sharing session and exhibit.

170

Notes: *Washouts are mysterious works, chiefly because they are so unpredictable and risky. There is just no way to know how your work will turn out once it has been acted upon by the water. It is generally a good idea, however, to leave some white spaces in your original tempera painting. This will give the ink a chance to dye some areas more completely.*

I have always reserved washouts for springtime, since they involve lots of sloshing and wet arms. Somehow the warmer weather seems the most appropriate time to conduct such an activity. Perhaps, because of the unknown qualities, kids always want to make a number of washouts. Thus, be sure you have plenty of space set aside for drying the paintings. There is little question that you'll see lots of imaginative results coming out in the wash!

Watercolor Fold Designs

Purpose: *To develop and refine a visual design from an unknown shape*

Materials:
White drawing paper (4.5" x 6"), watercolors, brushes, markers, plastic cups, water, newspaper.

Description: *All of us have spilled things or gotten spots on a favorite piece of clothing. Some of us who have taken courses in psychology may also be familiar with how patterns of spots are used in the Rorschach test. In this activity, we will be relying on the random effects of watercolor spots to launch unique visual designs.*

1 Start the activity by explaining to your students that they will be experimenting with watercolors to create unusual designs. The procedure is briefly described below:

a. Take a sheet of 4.5" x 6" white drawing paper, and fold it into two 3" x 4.5" segments.
b. Unfold the paper and begin to randomly and spontaneously apply your watercolors. Be sure that the paints are quite fluid.
c. After a few moments, refold the paper along the pre-folded line, and gently but firmly rub over the paper.
d. Reopen the paper, and your random watercolor design will appear. Study the design and decide what it suggests and how you wish to highlight it.
e. Use the colored markers to work detail into your watercolor design, and outline or add the things you wish.

After you have outlined the process and answered any questions, distribute the materials and let the chidren begin to work.

 Encourage each student to create several watercolor fold designs rather than one alone.

 When all the designs are completed, hold a discussion and exhibit.

Notes: *Watercolor fold designs are imaginative and fun. The watercolor section of the activity should be done quickly and boldly, while the drawing portion can take longer and be more thoughtful. The activity demands a high degree of imagination and sensitivity to the shapes and spots that are produced by the folding process.*

It is important to let your students make several fold designs and try to experiment with color and spot placement. This can be accomplished by applying the watercolor along the fold, on both sections of the paper, or only on one side.

This activity can also lend itself to an experience in poetry writing. After the children have completed their fold designs, ask them to write a short poem describing their creations. Just as the spots suggest diverse visual designs, they can also suggest amazing verbal ones!

Wild Creature Collage

Creatures from Collageland

Purpose: *To design a unique and imaginative collage creature from scrap materials*

Materials:
Colored construction paper and cardboard (9" x 12"), wallpaper and fabric, paper and magazine scraps, buttons, yarn, white glue, scissors, pencils, markers, crayons, sandpaper.

Description: *Collage, that curious art form where paper, cloth, and flattened objects are glued together to make a single composition, can be a great vehicle for formulating some marvelous creatures. Indeed, the varied tactile surfaces of different materials can suggest a particular type of creature. In this activity, we will be concentrating on making unusual and wonderful wild beasts who have never been seen before!*

1 Before starting this activity with your class, make sure you have an abundant supply of materials for your students' use. Scrap paper, old pieces of fabric, wallpaper, sandpaper, buttons, and yarn are all valuable things to have.

2 Bring these items to class, and hold a discussion on how different kinds of materials can often suggest different ideas. Explain that in this activity we will be making our own collage creature, and that each person should be as imaginative as possible. The creatures can have lots of legs or no legs, wings, propellers, or antennas.

3 Distribute the materials. Ask each child to select a variety of things and begin to arrange them on a piece of 9" x 12" cardboard or colored construction paper. It is important that the children experiment with the placement of the materials before gluing them to the backgrounds.

Once each child has decided how he/she wants his/her collage to look, they should do the gluing. Children can add extra details using crayons and colored markers.

Hold a sharing session and wild creature exhibition at the conclusion of the activity.

Notes: *It is always amazing what a piece of burlap, wallpaper, or rough sandpaper can suggest. Paper can be cut or torn to create fur-like effects, buttons can be added for eyes and yarn for unruly hair. Each child will think of many ways to do his/her own special creature, and all of these approaches are equally valid.*

Wild creatures have the potential of getting kids to stretch their imaginations through the use of varied materials. They are a fine way to illustrate the fact that those odds and ends, which we sometimes ignore, can be the basis of some very exciting things.

Wood Pendants

From Lumber to Jewelry

Purpose: *To create simple wooden jewelry from lattice strip*

Materials:
Several pieces of lattice strip (approx. 1.5" in width and 8' to 10' in length), coping saw, electric drill with small bit, sandpaper, manila paper (9" x 12"), pencils, colored markers, yarn (assorted colors), scissors.

Description: *Jewelry making is an ancient art form which appears in all cultures around the world. Although precious metals and stones are often used, wood is also a wonderful medium for creating decorative jewelry. In this activity, we will be using wood from the local lumberyard to make simple pendants.*

1 Before starting the activity with your class, you will need to travel to a local lumberyard and purchase an adequate supply of lattice strip. This flat molding comes in a variety of lengths and widths. I have found that buying two or three 8' or 10' lengths of 1.5"-wide lattice strip is a safe amount. This is the same type of lumber that one would use in constructing a rose arbor or trellis. In addition, you will also need a coping saw with extra blades and a hand or electric drill with a 3/16" bit.

2 Cut the long pieces of lumber into small 1.5" or 2" pieces using the coping saw. I usually prepare two pieces for each student in the class.

3 After you have finished cutting the wood, drill a hole through the top center or corner of each piece. Since the wood has not as yet been sanded, be careful of splinters. Place the drilled pieces in a bag, and bring them to class. You are now ready to introduce the activity to your students.

4 Briefly discuss the idea of making jewelry from wood, and explain that each child will soon be given the opportunity to create two pendants. You may wish to wear a completed pendant to class to increase interest. Pass out the 9" x 12" manila paper and ask each child to make several drawings for his/her pendant in pencil.

5 Next, distribute two pieces of wood and some sandpaper to each child. Caution the students to be careful of splinters, and ask each person to sand the wood pieces as smoothly as possible.

6 When the wood has been sanded, have each student transfer her/his favorite designs onto the wood using the colored markers. I have found that fine-tipped markers are most effective. However, be aware that the colors sometimes spread slightly when applied to the wood.

7 After the students have completed their pendants, pass out the yarn and scissors and have them string their works. String the yarn through the wood in the manner shown below. The pendant will now hang more evenly when it is worn.

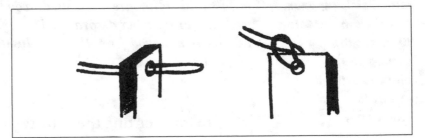

8 Hold a jewelry display session and exhibit, if a showcase is available.

Notes: *"Wood Pendants" are always an instant hit with children and are a fine way to introduce them to the art of simple jewelry making. I have found that the students not only enjoy creating these pendants, but they enjoy wearing them as well. In fact, you will probably find that each child will make as many pendants as you have wood pieces.*

These pendants also make excellent gifts and can be connected to holiday gift giving. Each year, my wife Eleanor uses this activity as a class fund-raising project. The students in her class make a great number of pendants, which they sell throughout the school for 25¢ each. The class donates the money they raise to a needy family or local charity during the winter holiday season.